Editor-in-Chief and Founder:
 Lyndon H. LaRouche, Jr.
Editorial Board: *Lyndon H. LaRouche, Jr., Helga
 Zepp-LaRouche, Robert Ingraham, Tony
 Papert, Gerald Rose, Dennis Small, Jeffrey
 Steinberg, William Wertz*
Co-Editors: *Robert Ingraham, Tony Papert*
Managing Editor: *Nancy Spannaus*
Technology: *Marsha Freeman*
Books: *Katherine Notley*
Ebooks: *Richard Burden*
Graphics: *Alan Yue*
Photos: *Stuart Lewis*
Circulation Manager: *Stanley Ezrol*

INTELLIGENCE DIRECTORS
Counterintelligence: *Jeffrey Steinberg, Michele
 Steinberg*
Economics: *John Hoefle, Marcia Merry Baker,
 Paul Gallagher*
History: *Anton Chaitkin*
Ibero-America: *Dennis Small*
Russia and Eastern Europe: *Rachel Douglas*
United States: *Debra Freeman*

INTERNATIONAL BUREAUS
Bogotá: *Miriam Redondo*
Berlin: *Rainer Apel*
Copenhagen: *Tom Gillesberg*
Houston: *Harley Schlanger*
Lima: *Sara Madueño*
Melbourne: *Robert Barwick*
Mexico City: *Gerardo Castilleja Chávez*
New Delhi: *Ramtanu Maitra*
Paris: *Christine Bierre*
Stockholm: *Ulf Sandmark*
United Nations, N.Y.C.: *Leni Rubinstein*
Washington, D.C.: *William Jones*
Wiesbaden: *Göran Haglund*

ON THE WEB
e-mail: eirns@larouchepub.com
www.larouchepub.com
www.executiveintelligencereview.com
www.larouchepub.com/eiw
Webmaster: *John Sigerson*
Assistant Webmaster: *George Hollis*
Editor, Arabic-language edition: *Hussein Askary*

EIR (ISSN 0273-6314) *is published weekly
(50 issues), by EIR News Service, Inc.,
P.O. Box 17390, Washington, D.C. 20041-0390.
(703) 297-8434*

European Headquarters: E.I.R. GmbH, Postfach
Bahnstrasse 9a, D-65205, Wiesbaden, Germany
Tel: 49-611-73650
Homepage: http://www.eir.de
e-mail: info@eir.de
Director: Georg Neudecker

Montreal, Canada: 514-461-1557
eir@eircanada.ca

Denmark: EIR - Danmark, Sankt Knuds Vej 11,
basement left, DK-1903 Frederiksberg, Denmark.
Tel.: +45 35 43 60 40, Fax: +45 35 43 87 57. e-mail:
eirdk@hotmail.com.

Mexico City: EIR, Sor Juana Inés de la Cruz 242-2
Col. Agricultura C.P. 11360
Delegación M. Hidalgo, México D.F.
Tel. (5525) 5318-2301
eirmexico@gmail.com

Canada Post Publication Sales Agreement
#40683579

Postmaster: Send all address changes to *EIR*, P.O.
Box 17390, Washington, D.C. 20041-0390.

Signed articles in *EIR* represent the views of the authors,
and not necessarily those of the Editorial Board.

The President Can't Do It Alone

EDITORIAL

What Are the Real Issues Behind All This?

June 15—The British have repeatedly assassinated American Presidents, after first assassinating the father of our Constitutional system, Alexander Hamilton. But you would have to go all the way back to Abraham Lincoln, to find the sorts of repeated threats against a President, especially threats of murder, that are being made against President Trump right now as you read this—under British direction. A "comedian" is circulating a photograph of herself on the Internet, holding up a replica of the President's head—severed.

At the same time, the protracted stabbing-murder of President Trump is being regularly performed before large audiences in New York's Central Park, under the proud sponsorship, and with the repeated vigorous endorsement, of the traitors at the British-loving *New York Times*—under the absurd guise of Shakespeare's *Julius Caesar*. The "actor" allegedly portraying Julius Caesar in this bloody farce, is dressed and made up to look exactly like President Trump—while his wife speaks with a Slavic accent and looks and dresses just like the President's wife, Melania.

Obviously, no one believes the *New York Times* that this represents "freedom of speech." It represents deliberate incitement to political murder, or even a license to kill—and that, even while an innocent U.S. Congressman, and another innocent man, are in critical condition in a Washington hospital, after being shot yesterday morning by a crazed mass-shooter looking for "Republicans" to kill.

Much more just like this could be adduced, as you all know.

The British Empire, whose bloodlust is behind all of this, just called this morning for Trump's impeachment, in its flagship *Financial Times* of London.

The reason for the parallel to the same murderous hysteria whipped up against Abraham Lincoln, is that the issues today are actually no less important now, than they were then. Then, it was the question of the survival of this Republic in the face of that same British Empire—a question which involved the future of the entire human species. Now, Lyndon LaRouche has made it clear that the victory of Jim Comey and Bob Mueller's FBI in their attempted coup against President Trump, would plunge the world into a nuclear war which would destroy our civilization and perhaps our species.

On the other side, the continuation of the Constitutional institution of the Presidency under the legitimate President Donald Trump—and the prosecution and conviction of the foreign-sponsored traitors who would wreck it—moves the United States into the "New Paradigm" for which Lyndon and Helga LaRouche have fought for almost half a century, by way of President Trump's open and sincere commitment to peace and partnership with Russia and China. We must restore Roosevelt's Glass-Steagall Act as President Trump has promised, as part of Lyndon LaRouche's "Four Laws" of June 2014, encompassing national banking, massive Federal credit issuance, fusion power development, and a full space program in an international cooperative effort.

The choice is now before this generation, before each of us, and before you personally.

EIR Contents

www.larouchepub.com Volume 44, Number 25, June 23, 2017

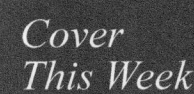

Cover This Week

White House at night.

White House photo by D. Myles Cullen

I. Truth, Lies, and Art

'Make American-Chinese Cooperation For the New Silk Road, the Heart of A Common Destiny for Mankind'

The following speech was delivered by Helga Zepp-LaRouche, on June 17, 2017, to a conference sponsored by the Schiller Institute in Detroit, Michigan.

Dear Guests of the Schiller Institute Conference in Detroit:

If you only believe the Western media, especially the mainstream media in the United States, you actually would have quite a reason to be pessimistic, because what do you see? You see an unbelievable campaign against President Trump, a color revolution. You have a special prosecutor who is supposedly investigating Russia-gate, the absurd idea that Russia stole the election from Hillary Clinton, and gave it to Trump, a special prosecutor who investigates possible obstruction of justice, and you get the impression that it's only a question of time when the presidency of President Trump will fail.

If that would be the only reality, it would be very bad for the people of America, and the world. For the people who have voted for Trump, which Hillary Clinton called cynically "the deplorables," it would mean that they still have one hundred million jobs lacking, because that's the actual figure which is not in the statistics, but that is the reality of unemployment in America. They would still have a dropping life expectancy rate, which is the surest indicator for a failing economy.

But this is not the whole reality: Because what the mainstream media are not reporting, is that there is already, right now, a completely new paradigm becoming a reality.

Schiller Institute
Helga Zepp-LaRouche

Less than four years ago, President Xi Jinping of China announced a completely new policy which he called the "New Silk Road." He did that in September 2013 in Kazakhstan, and in the almost four years since, this new economic cooperation policy, the so-called Belt and Road Initiative, has taken on a dynamic that is absolutely breathtaking. It is already now about twenty times as big as the Marshall Plan in the postwar reconstruction after the Second World War. And it is not limited by that, by no means: It is open-ended.

There are already six major industrial development corridors, in various parts of the Eurasian continent. You have more than one hundred ten countries cooperating, and it extends to all of Asia. It already reaches—despite the policies of the European Union, which is very hesitant, to say the least—it reaches into Eastern and Central European countries, the Balkan countries. Italy is cooperating, as are Spain and Portugal. France has a positive attitude. Switzerland wants to be a hub of the New Silk Road, and even the small country of Luxembourg now recognizes the advantages of this new policy. It reaches into Latin America.

But from my standpoint, one of the most important things is that it has changed the nature of the crisis in Africa completely. By the Chinese building railways, from Djibouti to Addis Ababa—from Uganda, Rwanda, Congo, Tanzania—reaching into the heart of Africa, it has completely changed the outlook of the Africans, in terms of a real perspective of overcoming poverty and underdevelopment.

The largest infrastructure project in history is now at least under consideration, in terms of a feasibility study: It is the Transaqua Project, which is the idea to refill Lake Chad, which has only ten percent of its original water at this point, and take some of the water from the tributaries of the Congo River and bring it along a system of rivers and canals, and this way, give hydropower to 12 countries which are along the route, bring in inland waterways, and provide plenty of water for irrigation of agriculture. So, it has completely changed the self-confidence of the Africans.

The View from China

There was, in mid-May, a very, very important summit in Beijing, the "Belt and Road Forum." There were twenty-nine heads of state, representing, together with other top leaders, one hundred ten nations. There were 1,200 international delegates. And I had the extraordinary honor to be one of the invited speakers, and I could both speak and make a commentary at the Think-Tank Summit, which was part of the Belt and Road Forum. And then, I had the opportunity to have high-level meetings, in Beijing, Nanjing, and Shanghai, in the following two weeks.

And from that very fresh experience, I can tell you: The world looks completely different from this perspective.

First of all, the delegates at the Forum had the very distinct feeling of participating in the shaping of history, of the creation of a new world economic order, a completely new paradigm of mankind, where geopolitics is superseded by a "win-win cooperation" among all nations which participate in this project.

Now, what is being discussed and being realized, here, is to export the Chinese economic miracle, in a win-win form of cooperation among all the nations of Eurasia, Africa, Latin America, and so forth. People from China naturally know what the Chinese economic miracle is, but I think Americans tend to underestimate it. It is really the greatest economic achievement in the history of mankind, and I think it goes even beyond the famous German economic miracle. Because in 1949, when the People's Republic of China was founded, because of the civil war and the war against Japan, the life expectancy in China was only thirty-five years. The infant mortality was twenty percent. The illiteracy rate was eighty percent.

Since the economic reforms of Deng Xiaoping, but especially in the last thirty years, these kinds of economic policies have created an economic miracle that is unlike any other development in any other country. It lifted 800 million people out of poverty. At this point, there are only four percent left in severe poverty, and it is the aim of the Chinese government to overcome and eliminate that poverty by the year 2020. The life expectancy has gone up to seventy-six years average. The illiteracy rate is only four percent; it is probably much less than that in the United States, at this point.

And China has become the world leader in many areas, but especially in the building of fast train systems, and it has already constructed more than 20,000 km of fast train systems, and it has the aim to connect every Chinese city by the year 2020 with a fast train. That will probably be 50,000 km of such fast train lines.

Now, since the Belt and Road Forum took place in mid-May, you have had, in rapid sequence, two other major international economic events. One was the St. Petersburg International Economic Forum, and then the Shanghai Cooperation Organization annual meeting in Astana, Kazakhstan. What you see in these meetings is the extremely rapid economic integration of the New Silk Road, the Eurasian Economic Union, and the Shanghai Cooperation Organization, and reaching out even beyond that.

President Putin just gave an interview, where he invited all Russian citizens to ask questions, and he got two million questions. One question referred to the cooperation between the New Silk Road and the Eurasian Economic Union (EAEU), and he stated what is very obvious: That this does not just improve the relations between Russia and China, but it is of global importance for the well-being of the entire civilization. President Xi Jinping has said the same thing many, many times, that what we are talking about is a completely new approach to world affairs, a community for a shared future of mankind.

Obviously, the key for this Belt and Road Initiative to succeed, is that the relationship between the United States and China must be going well, and they must cooperate, because they are the two largest economies of the world. And when these two countries can find a new relationship between each other, I am absolutely confident that there is no single problem on the planet which cannot be solved.

On Thursday, there was a very important high-level meeting in New York, which was addressed by, among others, the Chinese Ambassador to the United States Cui Tiankai, who basically gave us the story, that in history, it has happened sixteen times that a rising power was surpassing the existing dominant power. The ambassador noted that in twelve of these sixteen times it came to a war, and that four times, the rising power superseded the existing power.

He said that we do not want to have either the example of the twelve wars, nor the other four. What we are talking about is a completely new page in history, a true win-win cooperation—not a zero-sum game, where one wins and the other one loses, but a community of shared interest. In other words, that it is the key to what even many leaders in the United States have been warning about, that the United States does not fall into the so-called "Thucydides trap," which refers historically to the same problem between the ancient Greek city-states of Athens and Sparta, which led to the Peloponnesian War, and finally, to the destruction of the Greek state.

President Trump (@POTUS) on Twitter

President Trump said, my wife and I "are honored to welcome the President of the People's Republic of China, Xi Jinping, and Madame Peng Liyuan, to the United States." This picture was taken at Mar-a-Lago, site of the meeting of the two presidents, April 6-7.

The Real Reason for the Attacks on President Trump

Now, fortunately, with the election of President Trump, that danger is clearly very much diminished. There was a very good meeting in Mar-a-Lago, the first summit between President Trump and President Xi Jinping, earlier this year. As a follow-up, President Trump sent his advisor Matt Pottinger to the Belt and Road Forum in May. So this is on a very good route.

But let me just say, in parenthesis, that this very positive attitude of President Trump to China—and Russia, actually—is the real reason why there is right now the attempt of a color revolution against President Trump. It is because Trump is about to improve the relationship with Russia and China, qualitatively, way beyond anything in the past. And it is the political forces representing the old paradigm, those people who thought that when the Soviet Union had collapsed that they would build an unipolar world and keep Russia down, prevent the rise of China: It is they who have started what President Trump has called an "unprecedented witch-hunt" against his Presidency, peddling the absolutely absurd idea that it was the Russians who stole the election from Hillary Clinton and gave it to Trump. These are the same people who are now leading the charge that President Trump was involved in obstruction of justice, which is a complete lie. Even the *New York Post* came to the conclusion that the unbelievable hearing by the former FBI Director James Comey was really a show, which can only be characterized as "J. Edgar Comey," in a clear reference to J. Edgar Hoover, who used to blackmail Presidents and threaten them with the distribution of lies.

We should be absolutely aware: This is a very tense situation. It is not just what people now call the so-called "deep state," meaning the military-industrial complex, the intelligence community, in combination with the mainstream media. We should not underestimate the role of the British Empire. It was the *Financial Times* calling for the impeachment of Trump. It was the *New York Times*, which is supporting this disgusting performance of *Julius Caesar* in New York, where the main actor playing Julius Caesar looks like Trump, and his wife is dressed up like Melania Trump, and celebrating the death and the murder of "Caesar," every day. So, this is a very serious matter, but it can be defeated.

Privatization Won't Work

In order to make the collaboration among the United States, Russia and China successful, however, we cannot leave the cooperation in infrastructure on the level of private investments. The problem with private investors is, that they want to have a twelve percent return, per year, which is a completely wrong idea, in terms of the function of infrastructure. If Trump would just add it to the Federal budget, he would have the same opposition from the Democrats and the Republicans, which brought down the repeal of Obamacare.

The privatization of large infrastructure just does not work. There was an example in recent history where this was attempted and led to a complete disaster. I want to remind you of it and tell you about it, and that was when the Berlin Wall came down in 1989. We—that is my husband, Lyndon LaRouche, and myself—we proposed to take the "Productive Triangle," the region from Paris, Berlin, Vienna, which was no longer separated by the wall, beef it up through modern technologies, and then have infrastructure development corridors into Eastern Europe, to Warsaw, Kiev, and the Balkans. When the Soviet Union collapsed in 1991, we simply extended that conception to all of Eurasia, connecting the infrastructure corridors between Asia and Europe, and in this way, have the industrial and population centers of Europe and Asia connected.

This would have been the basis for a peace plan. It would have allowed the use of the industries of the Comecon for the modernization of the infrastructure of these countries with the help of Western technology, and it would have totally changed history for the better. But at that point, this was not the geopolitical intention of Margaret Thatcher, Mitterrand, or Bush Sr., and they went for privatization instead.

When the first part of the project, the Productive Triangle, was on the agenda, the chairman of Deutsche Bank, Alfred Herrhausen, had a similar proposal for the development of Poland, where he proposed to use the famous Credit Institution for Reconstruction [*Kreditanstalt für Wiederaufbau*] which had been the financial basis for the economic miracle of Germany after the Second World War. He was assassinated, and so was Detlev Rohwedder, who was in charge of restructuring the state-owned industries of the G.D.R., East Germany. He had come to the conclusion that he wanted to reconstruct them first, and then see what was socially acceptable, in terms of privatization. He was assassinated, and then, instead, they replaced him with a woman called Birgit Breuel, who went for rapid privatization. It led to a complete clear-cutting of the industry. The results are still to be felt today, because in the eastern part of Germany, there are still some towns and villages which are almost without people, because all the young people had moved away—there were no jobs left, and only those who were too old to move would stay.

The same thing happened after the collapse of the Soviet Union, when Jeffrey Sachs went for "shock therapy," and was able, in the privatization of state-owned industries, to cut the industrial power of Russia, between 1991-94 down to only one-third.

This had unbelievable social consequences. It led to a complete demographic collapse. Russia lost one million people each year in the 1990s under Yeltsin, and it was clearly a form of genocide, which was only reversed by President Putin. It led to the phenomenon of the "oligarchs," people, who all of a sudden were billionaires, without doing any work.

The same problem now exists for Africa, and the Africans are very clear: They say, this whole policy by the European Union to go for private investment in infrastructure in Africa will not work, because private investors want profit, and they are not concerned about the future for Africa.

This is why my husband recently called for the full implementation of a national credit policy, a policy in the tradition of Alexander Hamilton, Glass-Steagall, a National Bank, a credit system, and in this way *only* can America be integrated into the New Silk Road effort.

What has to be understood is that there are certain areas of the economy where private interests cannot play a useful role, becuse the projects create a framework for the entire economy. Infrastructure is not just measured by the cost you invest in it, or by the profit you get out of it, from toll booths and other such means, but the true value of infrastructure is obviously the entire transformation of the productivity of industry, which is made possible as a result of the productivity of labor power.

A Policy for the Future

What we are talking about is an entirely new economic platform, which is defined by a new level of technology. In this time, it must be absolutely fast train systems, it must be the maglev, and what the United States really needs, given the fact that they have only a miserable 150 km of fast trains, somewhere between New York and Boston—and these trains only go up to 150 km per hour—what is needed in the United States is about 40,000 miles of a combination of maglev and fast trains, integrated with urban metro systems to reduce the average commuting time, from presently up to four hours, to only twenty minutes.

The efficiency of infrastructure is all the more important, the more developed the level of production is. For many areas, industrial urban areas, like New York, New Jersey, Philadelphia, San Francisco, Los Angeles, or Chicago, or the greater Detroit region, or Cleveland, Ohio, I would suggest what should be taken as a model is the Beijing-Tianjin-Hebei model, which is planned to be turned into a super-city. It's called the "Jing-Jin-Ji

Xinhua

Above, Chaobaihe Bridge, which will connect Beijing's Tongzhou District and Hebei's Yanjiao County, under construction on November 27, 2016.

Right. a high speed train heading to Yujiabao Station leaves Tianjin Railway Station, marking the extension of the Beijing-Tianjin intercity to Yujiabao in Tianjin's suburban Binhai area.

Yang Baosen/Xinhua

I think, the biggest problem is: Do not just get stuck in the present problems. The infrastructure discussion in New York, as we saw it in the last couple of days: they don't have a vision for the future yet. They think about how to fix LaGuardia Airport; they don't consider that there could be population growth, or economic growth, or that with a fast train system, as we are proposing it, the function of airports would be completely different—so, maybe, you don't want to focus only on the airport, you should start with a fast train system as part of an integrated infrastructure system.

What we have to do, is to look at this whole question from the standpoint of the future, from the standpoint of a completely new paradigm of cooperation among nations. We have to start with the idea of one mankind, of a completely new set of relations among nations, where nations are not just looking for their own interest, but start with the interest of the other. That was the basis of the Peace of Westphalia, which has been the basis for international law and it is now the basis for the idea of win-win cooperation. Then, we can concentrate on the common aims of mankind.

What are these common aims of mankind? We can find cures for diseases, which are still incurable today. We can develop the idea of energy and raw materials security, once we think about the commercial use of thermonuclear fusion power. We can think about the benefits for every nation, in joint cooperation in science and technology, of space collaboration. And we can imagine many, many more breakthroughs, breakthroughs where we don't even know yet what questions to ask. That is the true nature of human creativity, that there are no limits to what human beings can accomplish.

We are still in the infancy of development of the human species. And I think we are very lucky that we are alive and can shape the future at this point. But I think the most crucial aspect for this whole perspective, to succeed, is: Make the American-Chinese cooperation for the New Silk Road function in the immediate period.

model," and it is supposed to take 130 million citizens, create one integrated new city of over 212,000 sq. km, integrate a system of airports, highways, fast train systems, maglev, and metro—so that for every person, it takes no more than twenty minutes to go from his house to his job. The trains should go about 200-350 kph.

In the case of the Beijing-Hebei-Tianjin model, there is a specific role for every city. Beijing is supposed to focus on technology and culture; Tianjin will be a research base for manufacturing; Hebei will have a core in minor industries. A similar approach should be taken for the United States, including both a renewal of existing urban areas, where the infrastructure is absolutely desolate, totally decrepit, but also the creation of entirely new cities, science cities, where centers for scientific and technological cooperation and international projects will be put on the agenda.

Why the British Destroy Shakespeare To Assassinate American Presidents

by Dennis Speed

O, my offense is rank it smells to heaven;
—Claudius, *Hamlet*, Act 3, Scene 3

June 19—"You are all Goebbels! You are all Nazis. This is Goebbels. You are all Goebbels! This is inciting terrorists. The blood of [Congressman and shooting victim] Steve Scalise is on your hands. Goebbels would be proud." The two protesters who interrupted the recent Central Park *Julius Caesar* performance, in which Donald Trump, as "Julius Caesar," is mock-murdered under the pretense of "poetic license" and "contemporaneity," made their trenchant view of the matter known, and the audience—their audience, for those 45 seconds—uncomfortable. That was the only properly performed drama witnessed by that audience that night.

Lyndon LaRouche emphasizes that the figure Casca, in Shakespeare's play, reveals the core of the real tragedy:

Cassius and Casca.

Cassius: Did Cicero say anything?
Casca: Ay, he spoke Greek.
Cassius: To what effect?
Casca: Nay, an I tell you that, I'll ne'er look you i' the face again; but those that understood him smiled at one another and shook their heads; but for mine own part, it was Greek to me.

Casca's arrogant ignorance warns us of what fate America must suffer, were we to refuse to master those ideas, essential to our continued durable survival, no matter how foreign they might seem to be. When President Trump, for example, invoked the American System of economy in Kentucky back in March, and Kentucky's Abraham Lincoln in that context, he might have usefully referred to Lincoln's habit of reading Shakespeare to his cabinet, as Lincoln often did during meetings of the 1861-65 War of the Rebellion ("Civil War"). He did this precisely so that he and they could think outside of the system of economic and social tragedy that he so eloquently portrayed in his Second Inaugural Address, a soliloquy more than a speech.

There is an unfortunate association of William Shakespeare with things British. It should not be so. The British rejected Shakespeare for over 150 years after his death, until the power of Friedrich Schiller's tragedies forced them to seem to embrace Shakespeare as an "alternative" to Schiller. In the case of criminal acts, including the use of a drama as the pretext for inciting a criminal act, an association between British intelligence-trained actors and assassins is a not only useful, but correct one to make.

Since before the beginning of the Trump Presidency, British intelligence has made it clear that it prefers to see Trump impeached or killed. The dossier of MI6 "former spy" Christopher Steele, which was the pretext for the launching of the Russia probe against the President and close associates, is a British intelligence product, as is the "Russia hacking" campaign itself. The inducing of a mass-agitation "Kill Trump" campaign in the United States, amplified by the gutter speech-like anti-Trump grunts of 15-plus "celebrities," is being coordinated (and probably directly) through American-based but British intelligence-connected networks under the pretext of a nation-wide "Impeach Trump" campaign.

The British kill American Presidents, and have been doing it since the assassination of Alexander Hamilton, the man that should have succeeded Washington in that office, rather than either Jefferson or Adams. Sometimes they use actors, including American actors, as collaborators and conspirators in assassinations, not only those less known, but even those that are famous. Lincoln is another example of a President felled by a British-deployed assassin's bullet. (Britain supported the South in that revolt against the Presidency known mistakenly as "the Civil War," and the nation of Canada was created 150 years ago as a way of preventing various of the Canadian provinces from joining the United States and becoming states.)

From left, John Wilkes Booth as Mark Antony, Edwin Booth as Brutus, and Junius Booth as Cassius in Julius Caesar, *in New York, 1864.*

John Wilkes Booth

Actor John Wilkes Booth and his successful assassination of Lincoln should be recalled here. Booth's meeting in Montreal in October 1864, six months before the assassination, with Jacob Thompson, chief of the Confederate secret service in Canada; his Bank account at the Ontario Bank, which still contained $455 at the time that he was killed; and his regaling of his Confederate friends and supporters in that city with readings from *The Merchant of Venice* and other Shakespeare plays, make it clear why Michael W. Kauffman entitled his 2005 book about John Wilkes Booth, *American Brutus: John Wilkes Booth and the Lincoln Conspiracies.*

So, telegraphing something like a live assassination operation against the U.S. Presidency by means of hi-jacking Shakespeare, and recruiting the credulous to yell in support of it—just as happens in the play Julius Caesar itself—is the inverse of the purpose of that drama, but is in fact an efficient means to build the "plausible deniability" pre-condition for the actual operation, whose true origins are to be ignored, even as they are displayed.

This is not the Classical notion or function of tragedy. "A great Classical tragedy is composed, and performed as a Platonic dialogue, such that the audience of that performance is placed, as in the intellectual balcony, overlooking that history on stage," LaRouche tells us in his essay, "The Coming Eurasian World." "From that higher vantage point, the audience is challenged to see the interactions of the figures on stage from a higher vantage point than virtually any of the depicted characters themselves. ...

"The players portray the action on the stage of real life. The author and players must reveal the system which controls the unfolding action, the system which controls the parts played, but which the individual participant in the real-life experience fails to recognize. Classical tragedy, so composed, so performed, is thus the model for imparting a true sense of history in both the ordinary citizens, or adolescents, and others. The pages of the historian's book, the historian's lecture before the audience, must aim for and accomplish the same effect; to bring the essence of real history, in the time and place it actually occurred, back into life within the mind of the audience, and of the historian, too. ...

"Such Classical drama, so composed and delivered, is the properly mandatory foundation for the education of all the actually qualified future citizens of a republic."

An audience, as poet Friedrich Schiller observed in

Dish Virol News

Senators stab Caesar (dressed as Trump) to death in Central Park performance of Shakespeare's Julius Caesar, May 23-June 18, 2017.

"The Stage Considered as a Moral Institution," should leave the theater better than when it entered it. The "Central Park Caesar," with its pornographic symbolic murder of the President, does the opposite. Cassius' famous statement: "The fault, dear Brutus, lies not in our stars but in ourselves, that we are underlings," once heard, should have prompted the audience to immediately empty the theater, were it understood. Instead, "it was Greek to them," the actors, and the director, and required the intervention's metaphor, "You are all Goebbels!!"—the only true poetic idea presented. No audience member was reported to have asked, "Are we the mob in Shakespeare's play?" that evening.

To become a qualified citizen of Hamilton's republic, skip Central Park Shakespeare, and the play *Hamilton* also, for that matter. Try staying home and reading aloud Treasury Secretary Hamilton's *Reports* **on Manufacturing, Credit, and the National Bank,** and its constitutionality. LaRouche's *Four Laws*—Hamilton's Reports but in a more advanced form—provide a new economic platform for America, which Americans

must no longer reject as "Greek to me." Small-group readings of the *Reports* and the *Four Laws* can ensure joint comprehension and mastery of these principles.

Lyndon LaRouche's idea of the republic, cited above, runs directly counter to the modern idea of tragedy, drama, and art in general. The United States is, thankfully, not a democracy. It is a Hamiltonian republic, with a Hamiltonian Presidency. And the comprehension of Classical tragedy will be the way out for the American people, causing them to accept, not Caesar's crown, but the olive branch of win-win cooperation that Xi Jinping and Vladimir Putin have offered the world, and the United States, as a way out.

Ad for Central Park performance of Julius Caesar.

Sylvia Olden Lee at Work

*The life of the arts, far from being an interruption, a distraction, in the life of the nation, is
close to the center of a nation's purpose—and is a test to the quality of a nation's civilization.*

—John F. Kennedy

*The following is an excerpt
from the book* The Memoirs of
Sylvia Olden Lee, Premier Af-
rican-American Vocal Coach:
Who Is Sylvia, *by Sylvia Olden
Lee and Elizabeth Nash.*

In 1992, Kathy [Battle] had
asked me to attend a rehearsal
which was to be filmed at 165th
Street and Broadway. Sony intended to release it in connection with Kathy and Wynton
Marsalis' planned recording of
Baroque Duet.

I was at Elvira Green's in Queens and had just
washed my hair when I got a call at eight A.M. "I'm
phoning," said Peter Gelb, "because Kathy would like
you to come today."

"Yes, " I replied. "I'll be there today at four."

"No," he explained. "She'd like you to be here at ten
o'clock. Could you come?"

"I'm in Queens," I said, "and my head is dripping."

"Would you please put it up and get in a cab," he
persisted. "We'll pay for it."

Elvira drove me all the way in, while I put my hair
up in curlers. I got into the apartment house lobby and
had to be announced."Yes," the doorman said, "you can
go up." So I got in the elevator, and the attendant let me
out. Then I rang the bell, and Kathy opened the door.
Out came a klieg light with a mike in front of it.

"Good Morning, Mrs. Lee, " she said. "Oh lord," I
muttered. With curlers in my hair and a scarf thrown
over them, I looked as if I had water on the brain.

"Oh, come in," Kathy added and helped me remove
the curlers.

With my hair still wet, I went in and sat down at the
piano. The men had left us alone.

"Well," I said, "I guess I can get my red pencil." I
didn't know we were being taped, or I would never
have said the things I did.

*Sylvia Olden Lee (right) working with Kathleen
Battle on Bach Cantata 51.*

youtube

Then Kathy announced: "I
want you to hear the Bach cantata 51, *Jauchzet Gott in allen
Landen* (Exhalt God in all
Lands), I'm going to do."

"What can I do at the last
minute, girl?" I asked.

"I just want you to hear it,"
she answered.

"You've done it, haven't
you?" I asked.

"Not so successfully, " she
answered, "Because I was
huffing and puffing. Too many
notes were dead, not vibrat-
ing." Kathy then sang: "Jahhahahah…"

"All right, " I interrupted, "would you go back and
praise God! You've got to be so enthusiastic because
you are saying: *Jauchzet Gott.* It's got to have the face
of Kathy which looks jubilant. Aren't you happy?"

"Mmm-hmm."

"You ought to be ecstatic!" After she finished, I said:
"Eighty percent. I'm so glad to get that, because you did
a lot. You do breathe where you have to, and every time
you breathe where you have to, there is another place
where you ought to, because you've got just as much
time. *Jauchzet*, breathe, *Jauchzet.* You ought to breathe
there. You know that."

"Yeah. I did take a breath there."

"I don't know. I didn't hear it." Make all the *zets*
staccato so it's not *Jauch\zet*. No. *Jauch zet.* Kathy,
what's *Jauchzet*?"

"Praise."

"How do we say praise?"

"Praise."

"How do they say that down there where you come
from in Portsmouth, Ohio, which is like Alabama?"

"Prai————se!" She gestured like a shout.

"Well don't you think Germans praise?"

I phoned my daughter in California and asked,
"*Loben* means praise, what is *jauchzet*?" "*Loben* and

preisen are 'praise', but *jauchzet* is 'yeaaaaaaaaaah'!"

So I said to Kathy: "You will have to sing this Yahahahahah with joy and praise in your heart, or it's going to sound like a vocalise." She sang yahahahahah with nothing happening. So we worked on it for about twenty minutes, and that girl works. If I had a trumpet, I would brazen forth that Kathy Battle has never been anything but sincere, generous, and totally devoted to whatever I had to do with her. She's a lovely, hospitable, though brilliant person.

After our session, we went in her kitchen. "I know you like orange juice, " she said. Then she brought out this empty container and handed it to me.

"Kathy, " I said, "there's none here." Now I wouldn't have said that if I'd known the television men were there with telescopic lenses and distance mikes in the dining room.

As we were sitting at the table, Kathy hummed a scale and said: "Is there a spiritual called 'Where did my voice go?'"

"Well", I answered, "that would be necessary for some people, but not for you. *Jauchzet Gott.* You know that, all right—show me how you are going to do *Jauchzet.* You realize you're singing about God now. Don't please me."

"I know, I'm all ready for the first one, and then I'm thinking how I'm going to get the 'G.'"

"One step at a time, " I admonished. So she sang: *Jauch———zet.*

"No," I said. "That's dead, because your face is dead. You got all the *Jauch* and the *zet.* Where is God?"

"I haven't gotten to Him yet," she replied.

"God, or *Gott* is just before you sing *Jauchzet.* You've got to think it right away, because you can hardly wait. You are so impatient to say it, you almost anticipate the orchestra. It's just jubilation! It's just exhalation!"

I never have to worry about her taking my criticism too negatively. Kathy knew that it didn't mean that *she* was dead, but that she's singing something in a "dead" fashion. These great artists have that confidence which comes from deep study, application, and meditation.

But I would never have said that if I'd known it was going to be on television."My dear," I would have suggested, "would you give it a little more of the life that we were working on just now?" I never thought this footage was for a broadcast to be shown both here and abroad. She had to approve every inch of that film before it was released, and letting me criticize her in that way shows what a great woman Kathy Battle is.

Then we went to the recording studio, and the musicians were warming up. I had never spoken to an orchestra, but there I'd been asked to offer some comments.

(Because Everett was a violist, I knew that after, they say: "Oh, hell, let's get the heck on out. Just play the music.")

"Gentlemen," I began, "please forgive me. I have a husband who was a violinist like you in New York City and got to be a conductor. I know that you are wonderful musicians, otherwise you would not be here on this job. They don't have time or money to waste on people who can't play this with virtuosity. Look, don't be sitting here sawing away and turning to each other saying: 'You think you'll make the 5:08 train this afternoon?' Don't be doing it absently. Now, I don't care whether you call Him God, Yahweh, Jehovah, or Allah, but think about Him when you are playing this introduction. You have thirty-two bars to introduce one of the most marvelous things ever written." It has only about four or five lines of words to it.

Although I didn't yet know him, I also spoke to Mr. Wynton Marsalis. "You, too," I said. "You've been talking about how you 'gave up some gigs to get your Baroque style back.' Don't stand up here doing 'doodle doodle doodle,' riffing. You've got thirty bars before Ms. Battle has even entered. You set the thing up for her. It ought to be so glorious and full of praise that she doesn't need to sing. Come here."

I took him to the window and pointed: "See that cloud out there? Your name is Gabriel. Now don't toot a note without thinking about Him."

When it was all over, we were listening to the rushes. "It's not happy enough," I said to Kathy. "Whether you are happy or not, you have to act as though you're one seraph up there with all those angels."

"That goes for all of us," stated Wynton.

"I think you are absolutely right." "Kathy," I added, "if you start the attitude two beats ahead, it would help us get it. If we could get you to just shake your head, go *Jauchzet,* and then look for God,"

"That's right," observed Wynton, "because I have to look for God too. And when you're here in New York City, you might not find Him."

"You don't have to look for Him," I exclaimed. "He's here, and you see Him. Praise Him!"

People have said that was wonderful. Is that anything great to say? Don't we all know it?

There will be a Centennial Celebration Concert in honor of Sylvia Olden Lee in New York City's Carnegie Hall on June 29, sponsored by the Foundation for the Revival of Classical Culture, in collaboration with the Schiller Institute and the Harlem Opera Theater. The website for the event may be found here.

II. National Infrastructure

GULLIVER TRAVELS TO MANHATTAN

Only LaRouche's Four Laws And China's BRI Can Solve Manhattan Infrastructure Crisis

by Diane Sare

June 14—Today "top experts" on New York City infrastructure were assembled to participate on two panels at the Crain's 2017 Real Estate Conference, ironically titled "Don't just think big. Build big." There was nothing big about what was presented there, except the gap between what was projected by the speakers and what reality is likely to be.

While admitting that the one-hundred-year-old rail, water, and other infrastructure is now being subjected to the stress of supporting many more people than it was originally built for and is reaching the end of its reasonable life expectancy, no one spoke of the potential looming chaos coming as early as July 10 when Penn Station tracks will be undergoing urgently needed repairs. Nor did anyone say what everyone knows: Since the entire transportation grid is already over capacity, there is no redundancy to allow for rerouting the

number of passengers who need to get into the city. New York Governor Andrew Cuomo is frantically trying to speed up needed repairs on the region's bridges and highways, in anticipation of a surge in automobile traffic resulting from closed rail lines, which could exacerbate the already hazardous condition of the crumbling roadways.

Because about 1.5 million people travel into Manhattan to work every weekday, the disintegration of the transportation grid is merely the most obvious of the crises. Look deeper, and one will find water mains that are the same age, or older than the subway tunnels, rats scampering merrily across neighborhood streets, record numbers of homeless people being placed in substandard housing, literally killing them, and many other crises. New York City has been looted by Wall Street and London, literally to the breaking point, where clos-

youtube   youtube

Left: A New York City subway platform under normal conditions. Right: Vehicle traffic on bridges into and out of Manhattan will increase greatly as parts of the aged rail network are shut down for maintenance.

ing anything for maintenance or repair threatens to collapse something else.

The first thing that is required, is to face this harsh reality and dispense with the foolhardy notion that just creating new glitzy buildings with bigger windows will allow human beings to survive. While not all of the speakers at the aptly named "real estate" conference were narrowly focussed on big windows, one left the conference with the distinct impression of having witnessed a group of supposedly well-educated grown ups playing in a sandbox where they made up their own rules and the outside world was not to be considered.

It is also necessary to recognize how the world has changed, even in the past four years, with China's Belt and Road Initiative, which is transforming large regions of the planet by increasing connectivity, and elevating the standard of living for billions of people, with high speed rail and water transportation corridors, among other great projects.

For example, a proposal was made by Jamie Torres Springer, Senior Principal, HR&A Advisors, to convert Rikers Island into more space for the already overloaded LaGuardia Airport. It wasn't clear from his remarks if the shortfall of "75 flight operations per hour" was the current statistic, or a projection for the year 2030, when 30 million more passengers are projected to be flying into New York, but whichever it is, converting Rikers Island from a "penal colony," as he aptly called it, into runways, would only add 30 more flight operations per hour—i.e. less than half of the demand. Springer also correctly stated that the waste-water treatment facilities in the region are over 100 years old and that billions of gallons of raw waste overflow annually. He proposed modern waste-water treatment facilities for this location as well. He closed by summing up the cost of this initiative: $22 billion, which he calculated could be covered largely by private investments and increased airline revenue, leaving about $5 billion to be covered with public funds, although he didn't express it exactly in that way.

He was followed by Chris Ward, Senior Vice President and Chief Executive, Metro New York, of the American multi-national engineering firm, AECOM, who spoke about the potential for development in the Red Hook area of Brooklyn. Ward showed a shocking photograph of the damage suffered in that area from

Marc A Hermann/MTA New York City Transit

Work on the Greenpoint underwater tubes of the New York subway system on Aug. 9, 2013, repairing damage from Hurricane Sandy on Oct. 29, 2012. These tunnels were flooded to a height of 15 feet. After emergency repairs got the line running, there were numerous shutdowns to replace damaged or destroyed equipment.

Hurricane Sandy, but only spoke about addressing the threat of future super storms from the limited standpoint of Brooklyn and Brooklyn's shore-front property.

It was not mentioned that in 2009 the American Society of Civil Engineers had dedicated a conference to discussing four possible storm barrier options for the New York City Harbor area, and not one of them was built, which would have greatly alleviated this disaster, and, obviously, a sane leader would be moving to get one or a combination of them built immediately.

All of the other speakers were at best similarly limited, or at worst completely delusional, expressing wild-eyed fantasies about glorious modern glass towers, and the money that can be made by renting them out to other similarly fantasy-ridden tenants, apparently whether or not one is even able to travel to them, or there is a basic sewage and water treatment plan in place to handle the new towers.

There are two major factors which have led to this sorry state of affairs, where generally well-intended adults were reduced to making sandbox-sized plans. First, the legacy of Bertrand Russell and the destruction of science over the last century, which has replaced actually scientific creative thought with linear deductive methods, which have nothing to do with an actually developing universe, as best understood and explained in the writings of Lyndon LaRouche.

Second, the problem that Glass-Steagal has not yet been reinstated, and the Four Laws of Lyndon La-

Rouche, namely establishment of a national bank and a system of Hamiltonian credit to fund those activities, such as fusion research and development, which will allow the American people to make a leap to a new platform of physical economy. Therefore, everyone starts his projection based on what he or she thinks can be paid for by the very practices which have already caused one big crash in 2008, and are about to cause another one any minute.

For example, as this author asked the panel, what impact would the development of high-speed rail have on the New York Metropolitan area? If Boston is a 40 minute train ride away, and Washington, D.C. and Philadelphia also? That is, if you can go from Washington, D.C. to midtown Manhattan quicker than you can currently travel from Fort Lee (New Jersey), to Fort Washington, New York, over the George Washington Bridge? And this is *not* even a bold future projection, since such trains already exist, over tens of thousands of miles of them, in China. We should be thinking about the next breakthrough beyond that. No one had an answer.

However, since such high speed rail could be built to service the busy east coast corridor of the United States, this does allow us to consider what would otherwise perhaps be unthinkable: maybe the only way to actually recreate New York City is to move a portion of the city to a nearby location. That is, build a new city. For example, the New Jersey Pine Barrens take up 22% of the entire land mass of that state. Even only a fraction of that, could sustain a new city of a million people or more. On a magnetically levitated high-speed train, they could travel to work in Manhattan in 15 minutes. One of the speakers proposed a "Staten Island City" of 300,000. Why not? Given the terrible overload on all of New York City's infrastructure, leaving no redundancy for shifting anything, it might actually not be possible to build what is needed without, at least temporarily, relocating part of the population elsewhere. People could have the option of returning to the modernized city later, or more likely, many of them might prefer their new location.

What Planet Are You On

Just about a mile away from this conference, another conference was being held at the Asia Society, entitled, "China and the U.S.: One Belt, One Road, and a 100-Day Plan" which was co-sponsored by the Asia Society Policy Institute and the China Center for international Economic Exchanges. The panel of very high level Chinese guests, including Chinese Ambassador to

Transrapid

The maglev from Shanghai to its airport.

the United States Cui Tiankai, was introduced by a somewhat transformed former Australian Prime Minister, Kevin Rudd, who had obviously been positively affected by his own participation in the Beijing Belt and Road Conference one month ago.

The first Chinese speaker, The Honorable Tung Chee Hwa, gave a short history of U.S.-China relations beginning with Nixon's 1972 visit. He closed by graphically citing the transformation of China from Oct. 1, 1949 when life expectancy was 35 years, and only 20% of the population was literate, to today, 68 years later, with 600 million Chinese lifted out of poverty, life expectancy is now 76 years, and literacy is over 95%. Both Tung and Ambassador Cui emphasized the importance of U.S.-China relations, not only in economic terms, but also that win-win collaboration creates the basis for peace and war avoidance, even in difficult cases, like that of North Korea.

China has not only self-transformed itself, but is in the process of transforming the entire Eurasian and African Continents. Ultimately, the Belt and Road Initiative will be successful only if the North American continent becomes part of it. Otherwise, imagine a great ocean liner, now finally able to access Port Elizabeth through the recently elevated bridge at Bayonne, only to be unable to unload or load precious cargo because the rail connection to Detroit has broken down. It is obviously in the mutual self interest of both China and the United States that the horrendous breakdown of our physical economy be quickly addressed.

CC/Ken Lund

The combined Port Newark and Elizabeth Marine Terminal in New Jersey constitute the principal container ship facility for goods entering and leaving New York metropolitan area and the northeastern quadrant of North America. It is the largest container port on the East Coast of the United States, and the third largest in the nation.

The China Investment Corporation has relocated from Toronto to Manhattan. It estimates that the United States needs about $8 trillion in infrastructure spending. They have already expressed an intent to invest $50 billion. But how? If we had a national banking system, that money could go into the bank and be lent out for great projects, with a multiplier effect.

How would the Chinese look at the Washington, D.C., Baltimore, Philadelphia, New York City, Boston corridor? With high-speed rail, these cities are not isolated fiefdoms, but part of one powerful region of the United States. From that standpoint, how should this area be developed? That would give us the proper perspective on how to solve the transportation disaster which is going to hit New York and New Jersey within the next three weeks. No smaller a perspective than that should even be considered.

What the participants at the Crain's conference put forward would cost about $45 billion. Imagine spending $45 billion on infrastructure whose function would be obsolete by the time it was completed!

What Universe Are You In?

In a recently republished 2010 paper, entitled, *What Your Accountant Never Understood: The Secret Economy,* Lyndon LaRouche addresses exactly what New Yorkers, and all Americans, for that matter, urgently need to consider, if they wish to survive: that Money per se not only has no value, but is not the metric of anything, except as a "medium of assigning uttered credit at a fair approximation of anticipated net physical cost (including a charge, over incurred direct cost, for sustaining a justified rate of margin for progress of the physical economy as a whole.)"

The point is that the progress of mankind, as measured by potential relative population density (how many people could be comfortably sustained per given area) and increasing energy-flux-density (which is what allows for increasing population growth with a higher and higher standard of living, as measured in physical terms).

What defines human economy is the anti-entropic nature of the universe, and the role of human creativity as part of that. That is why it is natural for human beings to wish to colonize space, and "do the other things," as President Kennedy said, "because they are hard." These things challenge us to become better than we are, and when we each become better, mankind becomes better. This is why an ambitious space program, and a crash program to develop thermo-nuclear fusion as a reliable source of power are so important to the successful survival and development of our species. It is also why participation in Classical music performance, Classical drama and beautiful (as distinct from ugly, violent or pornographic) art must be a significant part of our society.

Let us imagine Gulliver returning to his home in a manned colony on a distant planet, after travelling to present day Manhattan. How would he describe us? How would we rather be known?

Critical Infrastructure Funding: 'Washington Must Take Over This Crisis'

by Bill Roberts

June 19—Last week, responding to reports of various state-level, piecemeal efforts to fund critical infrastructure repairs and upgrades, American statesman and economist Lyndon LaRouche stated, "The federal government must take over this crisis; it is the only source of an orderly form of credit for this problem. This is a major national crisis; the U.S. economy depends on solving it."

After 16 years of Presidents Bush and Obama, U.S. infrastructure is decrepit, necessitating stop-gap emergency measures to prevent chain reaction, large-scale disruptions of productive, daily life for millions of Americans. The American Society of Civil Engineers, in its 2017 Infrastructure Report Card, has put the needed level of infrastructure investment at $2 trillion to be spent over the next ten years, or $200 billion per year, while chairman Ding Xuedong of China's sovereign wealth fund, the China Investment Corporation, told the Asian Financial Forum in Hong Kong on January 16 that that "at least $8 trillion" is required.

Private investment will not cover the broad spectrum of infrastructure investment required, since private investors will not invest where they cannot make at least a 12% annual return. Nor will the Congress ever agree to large increases in spending from the federal budget without gouging it out of some other program to maintain austerity.

Only the third approach, the Hamiltonian approach found in LaRouche's Four Laws, recognizes that only government credit issuance, not money, can address what is needed—large-scale investment in infrastructure and manufacturing, with an eye toward future expanded requirements that come with an upgrading of mankind's application of new physical principles, resulting in higher levels of per capita productivity.

Any other approach is simply suicidal.

Example: Great Lakes Navigation

Consider the situation on the Great Lakes, where large-scale transport of coal and iron ore form the backbone of the iron and steel manufacturing supply chain. If anything were to disrupt these supplies, the effects would be devastating. In fact, a report produced by the Department of Homeland Security in 2016 put into figures what the unexpected closure of one particularly critical piece of infrastructure would mean for the nation. If the locks at Sault Sainte Marie, Michigan (the

U.S. Army Corps of Engineers/Michelle Hill

At Sault Ste. Marie, Mich. on Sept. 16, 2011, the Burns Harbor *is in the Poe Lock (right) and the* Richelieu *is preparing to enter the MacArthur Lock.*

"Soo Locks")—particularly the 1,200 foot Poe Lock, which handles 70% of the cargo moving between Lakes Superior and Huron—were to shut down and remain shut down for more than six months, 11 million additional Americans would be out of work and steel production in the nation would almost completely grind to a halt. Specialized industries such as automobile manufacture—depending on a different alloy or "recipe" of steel for nearly every part—would not be able to continue to produce, even if a few steel mills with reserve iron ore could function for part of the shutdown period.

The lock is literally indispensable, as there is no adequate rail grid that could take the tens of millions of tons of ore annually from the iron mines of the Mesabi Range in Minnesota, near Lake Superior, to the steel mills elsewhere on the shores of the Great Lakes, and beyond. The Army Corps of Engineers, which manages the locks, admits that as time goes on, the likelihood of unexpected closure increases.

U.S. Army Corps of Engineers

The Soo Locks between Lake Superior and the St. Marys River.

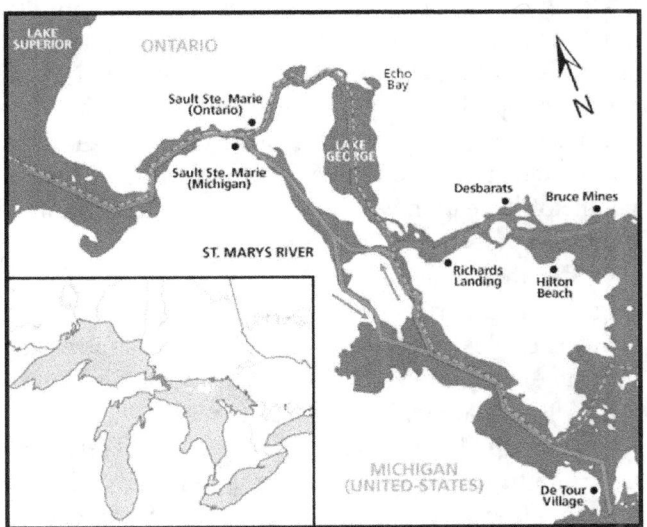

Passageway and locks at Sault Ste. Marie for ship traffic between Lake Superior and Lake Huron.

Surely someone must have noticed this and planned for the building of a replacement lock. "They" wouldn't let such a shutdown happen, would they?

In 1986, Congress, recognizing this vulnerability, passed legislation to construct a second large, modern lock where two unused, smaller ones are now. The project never materialized. Having authorized the construction, Congress withheld the funds. Over more recent years, more and more costly repairs have been made, but no major upgrades have taken place in 50 years.

Then in 2005, a cost-benefit analysis found that, supposedly, for every dollar invested in the new lock, a return of only 73 cents would be made. Incredibly, this kind of "revenue logic" made the project ineligible for federal funds.

Cost-Benefit Analysis: Who Benefits?

What should be transparently clear from this insanity, is that the future-oriented thinking that built the Erie Canal—that later led to the creation of a continuously navigable waterway from Lake Superior all the way to the Atlantic Ocean by way of the Saint Lawrence Seaway, driving the creation of the machine-tool sector of the nation—is a different species of thinking then that which controls the Congress today. That this particular cost-benefit analysis is considered to be flawed by shipping companies and is being redone, does not address the axiomatic flaw, namely, that the economy of a nation cannot be measured by the yardstick of a direct monetary measurement of benefit.

Abraham Lincoln, on the floor of Congress on June 20, 1848, took on this local-yokel mentality of judging the usefulness of a federal project in terms of the immediate, local payback at the point of use, citing the radiating effects of a "local project"—the Illinois and Michigan Canal that connects the Great Lakes and the Mississippi River—in lowering prices of commodities in states quite distant from New York.

David Lilienthal of the Tennessee Valley Authority (TVA; co-director, 1933-1941; chairman, 1941-1946) addressed the absurdity of such monetarist thinking. On the question of whether the expense to the American taxpayer for building the TVA was justified in terms of the benefits and values produced by the project, he concluded that much of the benefit of the project could not be measured by direct profit. The only such monetary return to the federal coffers was through the sale of electricity to consumers. The TVA did not account for, or record any statistics related to benefits that accrued from the improvement of navigation along waterways where the TVA had done its work, benefits expressed in increased shipping and increased consumption of commodities made more readily available, such as grain, oil, and gasoline.

In fact, many aspects of the benefits that came from building the TVA dams could not be measured in terms of direct payment to the TVA, including flood control benefits to down-river areas, but also the application, in regions not within the TVA region, of breakthroughs made by the project in plant food production and soil erosion mitigation.

In one of his books, *TVA: Democracy on the March* (1944), Lilienthal states, "But simply because they do not appear on the TVA's books as income, does not mean, of course that there are no benefits." (p. 39) He

US Army Corps of Engineers

A barge on the the final upbound passage through the Soo Locks before the locks and adjacent shipways freeze up.

immediately returns to this theme:

> The cost of such development work appears on TVA's books as a net expense; but the benefits appear on the balance sheet of the region and the nation. And, as with public improvement expenditures generally the country over, it was anticipated that such expenditures would be repaid to the taxpayer not directly in dollars, but indirectly in benefits.

In these passages, Lilienthal displays an understanding of the same principle upon which a Hamiltonian credit system functions. It does not function on the same basis as a private investment, requiring a direct profit on top of the return of the initial expenditure. In that respect, federal credit is superior, and not limited by mathematics, freeing the mind to consider how the people of the nation will benefit by a transformation of their condition and their activities.

After the stunning success of the May 14-15 Beijing Belt and Road Forum for International Cooperation, the boldest measure the Trump administration can now take is to implement Glass-Steagall and a Hamiltonian National Banking System, freeing the country from the grip of the Wall Street mentality and returning us to the trajectory of human progress. Only that approach, not private investment for local profit, can facilitate U.S.-Russia-China cooperation on the very highest level.

Every Day Counts In Today's Showdown To Save Civilization

That's why you need EIR's **Daily Alert Service**, a strategic overview compiled with the input of Lyndon LaRouche, and delivered to your email 5 days a week.

The election of Donald Trump to the Presidency of the Untied States has launched a new global era whose character has yet to be determined. The Obama-Clinton drive toward confrontation with Russia has been disrupted--but what will come next?

Over the next weeks and months there will be a pitched battle to determine the course of the Trump Administration. Will it pursue policies of cooperation with Russia and China in the New Silk Road, as the President-Elect has given some signs of? Will it follow through against Wall Street with Glass-Steagall?

The opposition to these policies will be fierce. If there is to be a positive outcome to this battle, an informed citizenry must do its part--intervening, educating, inspiring. That's why you need the EIR Daily Alert more than ever.

TUESDAY, NOVEMBER 22, 2016

Volume 3, Number 65

EIR Daily Alert Service

P.O. Box 17390, Washington, DC 20041-0390

- Only Global Solutions, Based on New Principles, Can Work
- Tulsi Gabbard Meets with Donald Trump Regarding Syria
- Robert Kagan Throws in the Towel, Complains U.S. Is Becoming 'Solipsistic'
- War Party Moving To Preempt Trump-Putin Reset
- Syrian Army Makes More Progress in Aleppo
- Duterte Gives OK to Nuclear Power for Philippines
- Europe Will Suffer from Maintaining Russia Sanctions
- Former Chilean Diplomat Confirmed, 'We Will Joyfully Welcome Xi Jinping'
- Duterte and Putin Establish Philippines-Russia Cooperation
- François Fillon, Pro-Russian Thatcherite, Wins First Round of French Right-Wing Presidential Primary

EDITORIAL

Only Global Solutions, Based on New Principles, Can Work

JULY 22, 2010

The Folly of Chronic Wars

by Lyndon H. LaRouche, Jr.

The subject here, is the issue posed by the repeated folly of the U.S.A., and other nations, in being drawn into "long wars," such as the post-President Kennedy "long war" in Indo-China, or the folly of the present long war in Afghanistan, the latter being that which I treat as a presently, leading case in this report which I present as bearing on the present quality of mental state of the administration of President Barack Obama.

In the matter of recent U.S.A. Afghanistan war-policy, I have not been an admirer of either General McChrystal's policies in Afghanistan, or of the probably worse case of the past and current policies of General Petraeus. Nonetheless; in everything I see, or hear of the interview with **Rolling Stone** magazine, McChrystal's conduct was neither unlawful, nor his criticisms unjustified.

However, there is a broader and deeper, leading issue posed by the behavior of the Obama Administration in this and coincident other present matters. The combination of several factors, including General McChrystal's remarks to **Rolling Stone**, including the news that former President Bill Clinton soars above President Obama in popularity, and including the pressures on President Obama to resort to lying, with evident hysteria, on increasingly crucial matters, especially on diverse leading issues posed by a U.S. economy now plunging into a collapse-phase, have witnessed President Obama as driven into a manifest state of mind which must be compared to a besieged Adolf Hitler's state of mind during Hitler's last days within the Berlin bunker, or the last phase of an "Emperor Nero"

Jimmy Carter Library

DoD/M.Sgt Jerry Morrison, USAF

The continuing long war in Afghanistan was launched by Zbigniew Brzezinski, as National Security Advisor during the Carter Administration, in cahoots with the British empire. The war continues today under President Barack Obama. It is President Obama, not General McChrystal, who ought to be fired, LaRouche writes. Shown: Brzezinski, in 1977; the Afghan War, March 2010; McChrystal, July 2010.

syndrome.

It was none other than President Barack Obama, not General McChrystal, who must be, most urgently, fired.

In the matter of the almost terminal state of mind of that President, the following relevant facts of the McChrystal case itself, are essential.

1. The recent U.S. continuation of the decades-long war in Afghanistan, is a continuation of a more than century-long series of "Middle East" wars first launched by the British monarchy during the last decade of the Nineteenth Century. This occurred, at that time, in the guise of imperial London's "Young Turk" operation, an operation which has been continued, to the present date, throughout the entire "Middle East" and adjoining regions, always explicitly, or implicitly, under the provisions of the infamous, Anglo-French imperialist, Sykes-Picot agreement.

2. This was, for example, the origin of Zbigniew Brzezinski's launching of the presently continuing long warfare in Afghanistan under the auspices of the U.S. Carter Administration, all done in concert with the British monarchy. This pattern was aggravated under President Obama, by his order protecting the British-owned and -controlled opium traffic spreading from a primary source in a British-protected province in Afghanistan, into Europe.

3. For the sake of purifying the atmosphere of certain crucially diversionary historical myths, it must be not only recognized, but emphasized, that this "Young Turk" affair, was part of the same continuing operation which had been launched, up through the present instance, with the initial assistance of that British Fabian Society's Frederick Engels who had launched the career in the closely related forms of both British secret-intelligence service direction, and British arms-trafficking operations of that British Fabian spy and weapons-trafficker, Alexander Helphand, the Helphand who also was, and is still usually recognized by name as the infamous "Parvus."

Much of "Parvus's" operations, prior to his role in the "sealed train" of Lenin's trip across Swedish territory in 1917, had been centered as in his role as a combined "revolutionary" and British arms supplier to sundry Balkan and related wars and revolutions. This continued in that form, until his crucial role in war-time Scandinavian operations, such as those of the Lenin affair of 1917, and his particular, earlier role in "handling" Helphand's British one-time "patsy" Leon Trotsky, an operation which must be seen as situated in the aftermath of British Prince Albert Edward's crafting of the 1894-1940 British alliance with the Mikado, against China, Korea, and Russia. This was the alliance which led into not only the Russo-Japan war of 1905, but lasted until the time the 1940 fall of France impelled Winston Churchill to turn for help from the U.S.A., thus breaking Japan's commitment to the alliance with Britain. Japan, nominally allied with Nazi Germany, fought the war against its trans-Pacific victims and other opponents, alone.

The crucial, thematic issue of this present report, is the outcome of that British imperial orchestration of the "Young Turk" operations, operations which, in this manner, for this and related reasons, are of the still-living character of all warfare and kindred manipulations by the British empire and its accomplices and dupes within the entirety of Southwest Asia, to the present day.

4. Although "cabinet-warfare generals" such as Petraeus and McChrystal, have their faults, however confused and misguided they have been, otherwise, McChrystal has remained, essentially a professional with an apparently deep commitment to his profession as a loyal citizen and U.S. military professional, however errant on other counts.

However, to compare either Petraeus or McChrystal to Generals Douglas MacArthur, or Dwight Eisenhower, would be worse than stilly, even obscene. Furthermore, within the matter of Generals Petraeus and McChrystal's part we must consider the stunning incompetence of their inherently ill-fated counter-insurgency and related "cabinet-warfare" schemes for the Southwest Asia matter. McChrystal appears to have followed the guidelines for his conduct with scrupulous attention to the letter of the law for generals operating in the kind of circumstances under which he delivered his remarks to **Rolling Stone** magazine.

5. The issue thus posed, is, that since the President of the United States, Barack Obama, had sent U.S. forces into Afghanistan with firm instructions not to interfere with the British Empire's opium production in a British-controlled region of Afghanistan, and since this arrangement created a hopeless situation for the U.S. troops being sacrificed to the cause

of what is fairly considered to be the President's treasonous role as such an agent of British international drug-trafficking interests: McChrystal acted under the moral obligation to do something to alarm the relevant institutions of the U.S. government to the effects of President Obama's British-dictated, and thus implicitly treasonous Afghanistan policy.

As far as he went in uttering what was reported by **Rolling Stone**, McChrystal did his duty as a commander in service of the United States. The fault, in this matter, was all on the side of President Obama himself.

6. The President had neither the proper grounds nor the means to carry out a politically successful court-martial of General McChrystal. General McChrystal's action has been proven to have been successful in its effort to cut down President Obama's already plunging popularity, all that despite the usual lick-spittles from the tradition of our own "yellow press." Thus, an important blow had been struck for our hope of rescuing our United States from the doom which the continuation of President Obama's evil reign would ensure. President Obama's reaction was chiefly the expression of a Hitler-like outburst of pique, perhaps even a sign that Obama's state of mind was now rapidly degenerating into something akin to a Hitler-in-the -bunker pique.

7. We must situate the distinction of strategic truth from the foolish, Goebbels-like babbling of the Obama Administration. To clarify the relevant features of the present strategic situation, it must be said, in response to what President Obama's follies have promoted, that we must interpolate a certain prefatory note at this point, a remark respecting the forecasts of Russia's illustrious strategic intelligence specialist, Professor Igor N. Panarin, for the U.S.A.'s future, into these prefatory remarks:

I have read an English-language, Dost Foundation summary of the reported argument by Professor Panarin. What I have read, thus, and from other relevant sources available to me here, lacks any formal error in Professor Panarin's particular suggestion that a breakup of the U.S. economy were likely before the close of present year.

Formally, there would be no error, excepting one of omission, in the implied set of facts on which Professor Panarin premised his argument. That crucial error in his particular judgment from early 2009, is his apparent lack of knowledge of relevant princi-

ples of Leibnizian-Riemannian dynamics which are specific to trans-Atlantic European civilization, most emphatically; we must emphasize the absolute difference in dynamics operating between the cultures of Europe, today, and the systemically contrary characteristics traced within our U.S.A. from the original New England settlements within the foundations of U.S. history to the present time.

The most significant element of error in Professor Panarin's 2009 paper, is in his presuming, in that report, that Europe generally, or Russia in particular, could outlive a collapsed U.S.A. The Professor's error features a component of lack of understanding of the principles of a science of physical economy, principles which are actually based in the Leibniz-Riemann tradition of dynamics.

At present, the center of the onrushing acceleration of a general, planet-wide, physical-economic breakdown-crisis, is within the British empire's central organization, the so-called "Inter-Alpha" group founded by Britain's Lord Jacob Rothschild in 1971, a group which has been constituted as a correlative feature of the same operation launched by London circles controlling key figures in the U.S. government in the matter of annulling the Franklin-Roosevelt-launched fixed-exchange-rate system.

The race is now on. For the moment, it were more likely that the collapse of the entire planet into a general breakdown-crisis would occur, initially, within the trans-Atlantic region as a whole, probably within western Europe, first. Such a collapse would be followed immediately by a "chain-reaction" collapse, similar to that of 1923 Weimar Germany, among all of the Eurasian nation-state economies.

It will be of interest to Professor Panarin, on this account, that he consider the fact that the root of the aspect of this global problem for Russia today, is the same London-centered imperial financier interest represented by the relevant controllers of both N.S. Khrushchov and Mikhail S. Gorbachov, controllers led by the Bertrand Russell school of early Twentieth-century, as later, "Cambridge systems analysis." That is the school which was the mother, for Britain's MI6, of such creatures as the Laxenberg Austria International Institute for Applied Systems Analysis (IIASA). It has been the policies of IIASA which played a crucial, treacherous, leading role in the collapse of the Soviet Union under Mikhail S. Gorbachov, and the same policies conduited into

N.S. Khrushchov's earlier role as General Secretary under the influence of IIASA spokesman Bertrand Russell's World Parliamentarians for World Government. In examining such influences, we meet the most virulent of the corrupting external influences on Russia's economic policies presently.

Today, that collapse of the entire world into what, unless reversed, would become immediately a new dark age, takes its root, not in financial matters, but, rather in the specific features of the collapse of physical economies caused by subordinating the physical national-economies to the reign of a presently hyper-inflationary system of speculation of a form comparable to 1923 Weimar Germany.

Unfortunately, if Barack Obama remains President of the U.S.A. past the Summer of 2010, then, the kind of disintegration of the U.S.A. which Professor Panarin projected in 2009, were a plausible estimation, although not a competent one scientifically. Thus, there are certain systemically mistaken presumptions, that of a reductionist error in method, expressed within the Professor's summary argument there; his conjecture errs in the respect that he does not take the Leibnizian definition of the Leibniz-Riemann principle of "dynamics" into account, and, therefore, he relies too much on inherently misleading, statistical-economic, monetarist considerations, through a lack of attention to the overriding importance of Leibniz -Riemann dynamics.[1]

8. There could have been, but for President Obama, a better outcome than that delivered by the decree of the real malefactor in the case, Barack Obama himself. The Senate should have been convened so that the U.S. Congress would hear, as a single body, what General McChrystal had to say. So, most of the panic-ridden members of the U.S. Congress, kissed the butt of our British-owned "American Nero," Obama, without risking the political-career hazards of their own exposure to the facts which General McChrystal had referenced in his curiously crafted interview with **Rolling Stone** magazine.

What is a general officer to do in such a situation, one like that fairly compared to a situation of an of-

ficer under the reign of the Emperor Nero? Why must we hope that that President will not be impelled to imitate his intellectual forebear, by imitating the Emperor Nero's action of last resort? Therefore, the crucial issue remains: the very continued existence of our republic, is immediately imperilled by each week which passes without actions to oust this President from that office.

Those facts taken into account, my assessment of the present existential crisis in our republic's very life, can be summarized as the threat of a case of another great nation, our own, brought to ruin by its own folly in being drawn into a foolishly conceived long war, such as that which our President John F. Kennedy would have prevented, had his role as an opponent of a long land war in Southeast Asia not been terminated by his assassination. President Kennedy had been explicitly opposed to an extended period of U.S. engagement in warfare in Southeast Asia. The presently ongoing long-war in Southwest Asia, was begun as what has been shown to have been a fatal booby-trap for the Soviet Union, a quality of past folly imitated currently by the Soviet Union's present heirs in the present setting of the same foolish behavior now continued by such as a foolish present U.S. government which has been duped by the drug-pushing British monarchy, all of which must be considered as a case in point against the presently impeachment-worthy Obama Presidency.

If we do not defeat the role of that depraved British puppet, President Barack Obama, in his mimicking of dictator Adolf Hitler, a mimicry which has been already copied as the Hitler-modelled, pro-genocidal health-care and related policies of this President, as also copied from Hitler by former British Prime Minister Tony Blair, we have reached such a point, that without the earliest ouster of President Obama, there is no visible future for any part of mankind, inside the U.S.A. itself, or elsewhere, at this critical global moment, now.

I. The Case of the Peloponnesian War

My recently published, leading writings, have frequently returned to the subject of the problematic characteristics of long wars. In light of the role of the present long warfare in Southwest Asia under the Anglo-U.S.A. reign of the U.S. Presidency of British

---

1. Although I do not charge Panarin with following in the footsteps of such adversaries of Academician V.I. Vernadsky as the typically British-influenced A.I. Oparin, Professor Panarin's method employed in his 2009 presentation draws its stated economic conclusions in a reductionist way contrary to the Leibniz-Riemann basis expressed by the principal achievements of the great Vernadsky.

puppet-President Barack Obama, the points which I have addressed on the subject of "long wars" earlier, should be recapitulated now for the specific purpose of conveying an understanding of the deadly implications of what may be identified under such titles as "The McChrystal Case," for our nation at this time. Therefore, I shall begin the body of this report, by reviewing the underlying implications of the historical phenomenon of "long wars," with the immediate issue of the Peloponnesian War in view.

Think of the present U.S. situation under President Obama as like "a new Peloponnesian War," as being echoed, similarly, by the "Seven Years War" of Eighteenth-century-ruined continental Europe, and which, also, established the British East India Company as an empire in fact, through the adoption of the February 1763 Peace of Paris.

To approach this subject-matter, we must prepare our examination of the roots of the world's present crisis with what many might wish to term "the deeply underlying" considerations in the attempted practice of an economic physical science, as I do in the present, opening part of this chapter.

It will not be necessary for me to lay out the full case on the subject of each of the periods of "long wars" here, since I have already done much to that effect in current publications such as my **The Secret Economy's Outlook**[2] published during the past month. The introduction of a summary of the following character will therefore suffice for use, on this present occasion, in defining the setting of this chapter's subject, the implications of the Peloponnesian War as a precedent.

I proceed now to a matter of relevant scientific defi-

To understand the continuing implications of the ancient Peloponnesian War, it is necessary to approach history as Bal Gangadhar Tilak (above) did in his considerations on the history of India, which he viewed from the vantage point of the Vedic evidence.

nitions essential for understanding the presently continuing implications of that ancient Peloponnesian War.

If we permit a distinction, here, between human archeology and "ancient history," we may date the appropriate notion of history as a science, to the study of the precedents represented by such exemplary cases as those of Sumer, or, of Egypt from the time of the great pyramid associated with the close of the reign of Khufu, or, the history of India as viewed from the vantage-point of the Vedic evidence treated by Bal Gangadhar Tilak's *Orion*.

This distinction between archeology and history, when history is strictly defined as a matter of principle, is demanded by regard for access, or want of access to those defining qualities of the individual human mind which were examined in exemplary fashion by the dialogues and related literary products of Plato. That is to say, that we must rise above the assumptions associated with the primitive outlook represented by the erroneous, but wide-spread, statistical belief in the evidence of mere sense-certainty. Or, let us agree, that that better approach chosen by me here, may be emphasized by examining the distinction between the reality of the archeological fact of the siege of Troy, and that insight into the Classical Greek legacy epitomized by the method employed in the dramas of Aeschylus and the works of Archytas and his associate Plato.

True knowledge of history begins when the ironies of the pair-wise and kindred interactions of the mental processes among individuals are accessible to our knowledge. Otherwise, we are left to infer history from study of the footprints which a society has left behind in its passing.

I have set forth crucial indicators of the basis for proposing, even demanding that distinction, in such notable locations as my already referenced, recently pub-

2. See **EIR**, July 16, 2010 http://www.larouchepub.com/lar/2010/3727secret_econ_outlook.html

lished **The Secret Economy's Outlook**. We must escape from the misleading, conventional notions of a mind governed by the mere products of sense-certainties, a feat which which must be accomplished by discovering the reality of the higher domain of Leibniz-Riemann dynamics, a subject which is represented most conveniently for this occasion, by those powers of the Classical imagination typified, for the English-speaking scholar, by the treatment of the specifically ontological principle of metaphor which I associate with my own joyous reading of the freshly minted, 1947 edition of William Empson's *Seven Types of Ambiguity*.[3]

For the native English-speaker of Classical artistic practice, the most appropriate choice of approach for English speakers, is, thus, that to be met in Percy Bysshe Shelley's *A Defence of Poetry*.

In Shelley's England

It is notable, for our purposes here, that Shelley's *A Defence of Poetry* is ironically dedicated to Thomas Love Peacock, not to be confused with the celebrated George Peacock who typifies the legacy of a trio of three young scholars from Cambridge's Trinity College. The second member of that trio, was the future leading astronomer of England, the figure later to become known as Sir John Herschel; the third, was Charles Babbage (the future inventor of the root-principle of design of operations of a modern digital computer).[4] Notably, George Peacock had gone on from scientific training, to becoming, among other professions, a notable English clergyman, and an acquaintance of Shelley. The three Cambridge youngsters of that time at Trinity, combined to translate LaCroix's

Differential and Integral Calculus, and more, into English, an act which upset the Newtonian hacks of Cambridge, I would say, " deliciously," at the time. The trio typifies the best of England at that time.

Reference to that trio's work at Cambridge can serve our mission here, as illustrating the true connection between a creative method of physical science, and the non-mathematical notions which are indispensable for an actually scientific approach to the role of creative mental processes, in contrast to an appropriately subordinated department of those mathematical operations in the work of David Hilbert or of the far worse Bertrand Russell traditions.

Contrary to the sundry varieties of the statistical reductionists, really competent science has never been properly separated from Classical artistic composition. The principles of the Classical artistic imagination, as referenced by Shelley in his *A Defence of Poetry*, are to be approached from that relevant, higher standpoint which I have emphasized within the pages of **The Secret Economy's Outlook**, where I treat the essential principle of all true creativity, including that of Classical artistic composition and physical science alike.

That identifies the point of the connection of William Empson's ontological definition of a principle of metaphor to the examination of those creative mental powers common to Classical artistic composition and true physical science.

I restate that principle itself as I presented it in my **The Secret Economy's Outlook**, as follows.

On the Human Mind

What we regard as the individual human mind, has two distinct, but interrelated aspects. The first, the more familiar, is the aspect of mental life associated within the bounds of a systemically mistaken presumption, that sense-perceptions are simply echoes of the presumed mathematical form of physical reality of the universe. The needed correction of that terribly mistaken view, is demonstrated with extraordinary forcefulness, and in the most notable way, by Johannes Kepler's uniquely original discovery of the principle of universal gravitation, as contained within the full text of his *Harmonies*. This is echoed by Albert Einstein's emphasis on the fact that the universe as defined implicitly by Kepler's actual discovery of a principle of gravitation, is a universe which, as Albert Einstein emphasized, is always finite, but without boundary.

That means that universe is not a permanently fixed

---

3. Shelley's *A Defence of Poetry*, which may very well echo the international influence of Friedrich Schiller intentionally, or in other ways, echoes the metaphysics of modern physical science associated with the tradition of Cardinal Nicholas of Cusa, but which harks back to the pre-Aristotelean Classical scientific tradition of Plato, in particular. That principle is intrinsic to the actually creative impulse of competent scientific discoveries of principle, as is strongly suggested by Albert Einstein's loving relationship to his violin.

4. It should be said, that Charles Babbage's final stage of design of his series of Calculating Engines, was the forerunner of what emerged during the post-World War II period as the conceptual root of the design of the Remington-Rand and IBM computer designs. All that remained needed, were the advances in machine-tool design which became available as adequate to realize the intention in Babbage's own achievement. Any designer of the systems operable over the course of the 1950s and slightly beyond, would recognize much in reading the most advanced stage of Babbage's designs.

creation, but is a continuing, ontological process of creation, as Philo of Alexandria had denounced the contrary opinion of Aristotle on this account. Aristotle's own fraudulent argument was later echoed by Friedrich Nietzsche's modern re-assertion of the corollary of Aristotle's dictum, "God is dead."

Thus, in competent principles of physical science, mathematics is a language of mere shadows, such that competent science depends upon the superseding of putatively fixed systems by the application of that same real-life, real-universe principle of creation, a principle which William Empson identified as metaphor.

This distinction shared by competent physical science and Classical artistic composition, is made explicit by any competent form of scientific reading of Kepler's *Harmonies*.

Thus, Kepler's solution proceeds from the recognition that the principle of gravitation can be efficiently adduced only by what Empson identified as the principled concept of metaphor, by emphasizing the contradictory character of what might be mistaken for what are often taken to be the apparently ontological implications of such notions of sense-perception as those of sight and heard harmonies. More to the point, all valid kinds of universal physical principles echo, in the method of their discovery, the method employed by Kepler in his discovery of a universal principle of gravitation. That method is the same thing, ontologically, as Empson's conception of metaphor.

With discoveries of principle akin to what I have referenced here as that discovery by Kepler, that individual human mind which is aware of this fact of experimental evidence, is impelled to acknowledge that which is called belief in sense-certainty, tends to mislead the victims of such ontological misbeliefs into a false-to-truth notion of physical science itself.

We are, therefore, properly impelled, in this way, to emphasize that sense-certainties are actually knowable phenomena only to the degree that we rise to the ability

Institut International de Physique Solvay

The Riemannian genius of Einstein and Planck, or Mendeleyev, or Pasteur, is opposed to that evil variety of so-called "mathematical physicists" associated with the 1920s romp of the obscene Bertrand Russell and his accomplices during the period of the 1920s Solvay Conferences. Shown: the 1927 Solvay Conference; Einstein is seated front row, center. Planck, three seats to his left.

to cope with the reality that what appear to be sense-certainties are, in reality, only shadows cast, as by an unseen, but efficient reality, upon the universe of our experience of actually creative forms of the physical action of qualitative, rather than merely quantitative changes. Such is the proper definition of true, universal discoveries of universal physical principle.

Reductionism as a Mental Illness

The success of the individual's progress in the direction of gaining that critical insight, points our attention to the poisonous effects of that sort of incompetence which is expressed as blind faith in the reductionist's notion of a purely mathematical notion of physics.[5] On that point, we are confronted with the fact of the existence of the qualitatively higher than mathematical quality of the scientific-creative, and related creative powers of the human mind, a quality of knowledge which is achieved only through ascent, above and beyond mathematical systems as such, to the notion of a universe premised upon a universal, metaphorical principle of physically efficient human creativity, as

---

5. For example, the derivatives of the dogma of Paolo Sarpi, and of such products of Sarpi's influence as the economic and related doctrine of Adam Smith.

shown in the language of Nicholas of Cusa's *De Docta Ignorantia*. This is what is to be recognized, for convenience, otherwise, as the common principle of the creative imagination, the principle which permeates the work of Leibniz and Bernhard Riemann's discoveries – as the fact of the existence of what should be intended by reference to the ontological conception of the human soul.

The phenomenon to which Shelley brings the reader in the closing paragraphs of his *A Defence of Poetry*, is just that. Gottfried Leibniz had defined this, during his work of the 1690s, as that principle of *dynamics*, which he attributed to the precedent of the Classical Greek conception known as *dynamis* to such figures as Archytas and Plato.

For example, take the exemplary case of the discovery of the inherently anti-Euclidean principle of the catenary by Filippo Brunelleschi, the principle which Brunelleschi employed for the crafting of the cupola of Florence's **Santa Maria del Fiore**, which was the only practical means available to Florence at that time, for that task of construction. This and related, namely "anti-Aristotelean" discoveries in the practice of a physical geometry (rather than childish academic credulities), as extended by the Leibniz-Jean Bernouilli development of the physical principle of least action, has illustrated what became the crucial point of principled difference between the true Riemannian genius of an Einstein and Planck, or Mendeleyev or Pasteur, as opposed to all among that pestilence of what are merely, a-prioristically mathematicians, such as David Hilbert, or, the actually evil variety of so-called "mathematical physicists" associated with the 1920s romp of the obscene Bertrand Russell and his accomplices during the period of the 1920s Solvay Conferences.

The pattern of reductionist ideology which I have just pointed out in the immediately preceding paragraphs, must be recognized as a systemic expression of mental illness. Not only is that the case, but this is both the most significant of all forms of mental illness—the virtual mother of the evil which is virtually all related mental dysfunctions, and is also a principal root of all other leading forms of mental illness in societies known to history up to this present time.

I explain that point summarily, as follows.

As I have both stated and emphasized within a series of published works during the course of 2009 and 2010 to present date, those actually creative functions which distinguish human individuals from beasts, lie outside the realm of sense-perceptual certainties, such as the implicit insanity of belief in a formal mathematical physics, as distinct from, for example, the modern physical chemistry of a Louis Pasteur, Mendeleyev, Max Planck, Albert Einstein, William Draper Harkins, or Academician V.I. Vernadsky. In other words, as Kepler's uniquely original discovery of gravitation attests, and as Albert Einstein identified that proof of principle as defining a physical universe as being both finite and yet without bounds, sense-certainties are, at their relatively very best, no better than mere shadows cast upon the field of mere opinions, both seen as if cast by the hand of an unseen reality.

That means, among other connotations, that the proper (which is to say, "sane") personal sense of identity, locates sanity in the developed ability of the individual human mind to locate his, or her personal identity as a substance located "as if from above," not to be part of the class of "those mere shadows of reality" which are the quality of all notions of sense-perceptual experience as such.

That distinction is the appropriate referent for the notion of an implicitly immortal, rather than merely "material" human "spiritual" being, a notion which is the only truly human sense of a valid, healthy sense of personal identity. That is the only true and sane notion of individual personal identity, and of the healthy forms of social relations among persons who have gained access to that higher conceptual standpoint for regarded experience.

This distinction is, for example, precisely that of the potential represented by that form of personal individual sanity. That is a quality which is expressed in a notable degree by the genius of Albert Einstein and others like him, or the great Cardinal Nicholas of Cusa, on this same account. It is within this specific domain of what we know as mental practice, that all true physical science and Classical artistic composition find their true place of residence. It is the domain which the ancient Pythagoreans identified by *dynamis*, which Gottfried Leibniz defined as dynamics during the 1690s, which is the source of the same social effect which Shelley identified in the concluding paragraphs of his *A Defence of Poetry*.

There is, in short, a social process which is mediated by the mere shadows of sense-perceptual experience, but which is not contained within it. It is also the medium with which Plato confronts such implicitly reductionist fools as the character of Parmenides and his modern likenesses.

This distinguishes the higher quality of intellectual domain which allows the inhabitant of such qualities to cope, conceptually, with the otherwise ontologically incomprehensible realities of a universe composed according to the notion of cosmic radiation as primary. It is the state of mind of a future culture of humanity which has then developed, among at least some of its members, the qualities of mind needed for mankind's future adaptation to conditions such as those to be found in future successful return flights from our Moon to Mars, and back.

The Apollo cult intervened, despite the warnings of such prophetic dramatists as the great Aeschylus, to plunge Greece into the orgy of destruction of the Pelopponesian long war (432-404 B.C.). Shown: The "Apollo Belvedere"; the ruins of the Temple at Delphi, seat of the Cult of Apollo.

Science, Sociology & War

Once the ancient notion of *dynamis* is compared to Leibniz's uniquely original, modern definition of dynamics, we become equipped to reckon competently with the quality of social phenomena met in the expression of systemic social conflicts, as characteristic expressions of both the interior of nation-state and comparable cultures, and among them. Begin our study of this matter with what I have already indicated as this chapter's particular subject-matter, the case of the infamous Peloponnesian War, as follows.

Consider what should have been taken as a forewarning of both the Peloponnesian War itself, and of the aftermath of the failure of the Greeks to follow Plato's intention to destroy his target, and, thus, overturn the folly of the Peloponnesian War, which should have been done by crushing the Mediterranean imperial maritime power vested in the intrinsically evil cult of the Delphi cult of Apollo.

It is now time to recall, today, that the naval victory over Persian imperial forces by the combined forces of what we customarily reference as "the ancient Greeks" today, not only rescued Greece from the earlier, prolonged efforts of the so-called Persian Empire to destroy Greek sovereignties, but created what turned out to have been a wasted opportunity: an opportunity largely wasted through the folly of the Peloponnesian War, for cooperation among the forces of those Greeks and Egypt for a cooperative step forward among the nations and peoples of the Mediterranean maritime littoral.

However, the same Apollo cult which had claimed, earlier, that it had been the power which had destroyed the kingdom of the fabulously rich King Croesus, intervened, despite the warnings of such prophetic dramatists as the great Aeschylus, to plunge Greece into an orgy of destruction of a type, like that of the Seven Years War, later. This was a development which we must recognize as virtually the same quality of strategic significance of that so-called "Seven Years War" through which the British East India Company secured its victory as an empire under the leadership of Lord Shelburne, thus launching what has remained as the world's British Empire from that day in 1763, to the present time of the fag end of the British monarchy's use of Lord Jacob Rothschild's imperial Inter-Alpha group of leadership of approximately seventy percent of the world's eminently bankruptable, reigning international banking power of the world today.

Similarly, it was through the folly of the succession of the French Reign of Terror and Napoleon Bonaparte's re-enacting the precedents of such follies of both the Peloponnesian War and that of the mid-Eighteenth-century "Seven Years War," that the British Empire was enabled to reduce those same great European nations who had, earlier, enabled our American victory in 1782, which were now to fall into a nearly ruined condition during a subsequent time, until the global, revolutionary effects of that great victory over the forces of the British Empire which had been led by U.S. President Abraham Lincoln.

It was, similarly, the success in the mid-1870s of the U.S.A.'s influence in such continental European powers as Bismarck's Germany and Russia's mightily successful programs of the great Russian statesman Count Witte and the great scientist Dmitri Mendeleyev, which were typical of those developments which drove the British monarchy to the desperation of forcing the dumping of Bismarck by the British royal family's German Kaiser, and trapping Germany, thus, into a war aided by Britain's ally Japan, in Japan's attack on China, Korea, and Russia, wars which prepared the way for setting off the so-called "great war" of 1914.

Similarly, we have the case of that assassination of U.S. President John F. Kennedy, which removed the President Kennedy who had been a stubborn obstacle to Britain's intention for launching a long U.S.A. war in Indo-China, a long war which destroyed the United States to such a degree of British imperial advantage by the 1968-1971 interval, that our U.S.A. was soon transformed, since the Nixon and Carter administrations, into what had been described during the time of Secretary of State John Quincy Adams as the status of "a mere cock boat in the wake of a British man o' war," as, again, since from 1971-72, to the present day.

This British system was, essentially, not really a new kind of expression of imperialism during any part of the interval of world history between the Peloponnesian War, and the ever-worse degree of ruin of our republic by its being suckered, again and again. So, in a similar way, our republic was being ruined, following the catastrophe which was the post-Kennedy, 1964-1975 decade of the U.S. Indo-China War, through the time of the presently ongoing, British-orchestrated U.S.A. military follies of a far worse than merely foolish U.S. President Obama in Southwest Asia. This trend is still, presently continuing through the follies of London's launching of Iraq wars, a virtually continuing, long Afghanistan war, and a series of regional wars, under the influence of the British "Sykes-Picot" control over some very, very foolish Israelis, a certain, presently reigning faction among Israelis whose folly is presently expressed as an immediately threatened nuclear-weapons assault on Iran.

This disaster of repeated follies of "divide and conquer," has been a copy of the practice of, in principle, the ancient Roman Empire. This was the folly practiced by Byzantium after Rome. This was the chronic state of recurring European periods of religious warfare, from the period 1492-1648, which Venetian maritime and monetarist power set off in the effort to crush the successes of the Great Ecumenical Council of Florence, such as that launching of modern European science by the initiatives of such geniuses as Filippo Brunelleschi and Cardinal Nicholas of Cusa.

Must we not ask ourselves: "What is the root of such a persistently recurring, criminal folly of entering into wars and kindred conflicts which are crafted as means for breaking the power of duped, formerly sovereign governments?" Why are governments and peoples so stupid, even stupidly evil, as to engage in such forms of traps of warfare as are typified by the case of the Peloponnesian War, or in the opium-pit of Afghanistan presently?

Machiavelli's Genius

To restate the same issue in a slightly different manner: "What has been the motive for the extent of the lying defamation against one of the greatest strategists representing the true republican cause, the great Niccolo Machiavelli?"

Said briefly: Machiavelli was, essentially, a follower of the great Leonardo da Vinci who had been driven out of Italy, into a place of relative safety, Amboise, in France. Machiavelli had been a middle-ranking, but important official of the Republic of Florence, who was virtually imprisoned and crippled in his freedom by those victorious forces which had crushed the Republic of Florence. He remained such a republican throughout the remainder of his life, and earned the respect, as by all the best professional officer cadres of the modern world, until the period of the U.S. Indo-China war, a Machiavelli who has been one of the founders of modern strategy, always emphasizing the republican cause in seeking arts for dealing with the pestilence of oligarchy and oligarchism polluting all of Europe during his own part of the 1492-1648 religious warfare.

Why was Machiavelli defamed in the manner used against him?

To state the point in the simplest terms: simply said, the oligarchical parties of Europe feared the infectious power of competence expressed by Machiavelli's mind, and hated him on that account (as many in certain leading circles of the world express a similar, deadly fear of me). Chiefly, the oligarchically inclined powers of the modern world, then as now, especially the financial oligarchy typified by Venice, still, to the present day, like their medieval and ancient predecessors, fear nothing as much as the very existence of the leaders in any nation who admire a constitution which converges on the intention of our own republican form of Federal Constitution. The standpoint of our President Franklin Roosevelt, or Abraham Lincoln before him, is what the oligarchs of the world, including our Wall Street brigands and vaulted Bostonians, hate and fear with a brutishly mouth-frothing rage.

The motive for the lying defamation against Nicolò Machiavelli (1469-1527), a follower of Leonardo da Vinci, was his commitment to the republican cause vs. the pestilence of oligarchy that polluted all of Europe during his lifetime, and throughout the 1492-1648 religious wars.

Such types as those still today, would also hate Machiavelli to the extent that they actually sensed the specific efficiency of his work.[6]

That much said to describe the global setting within which our view of known history is staged, consider the essential implications of the Peloponnesian War itself.

What Is Imperialism, Actually?

As I have emphasized a short space above, the great folly to be studied in trans-Atlantic civilization, still today, has been the continued toleration of a weakness expressed in the ability of powerful empires to induce the intended victim-nations to quarrel among themselves, to such an effect as we witness in the case of the mid-Eighteenth-century "Seven Years War," in the similarity of the effect of the folly of the Napoleonic wars, and, so, case by case, following that 1763 precedent, as to "World War One," or, in Winston Churchill's launching of that "Cold War" which ruined both the U.S.A. and western and central Europe, almost as much as it did the Soviet Union in the end. So, we have enjoyed the infernal epidemic of worse than useless, bleeding

wars and kindred diversions, which have continued the pattern of folly set into motion by those later wars which had been made possible by the assassination of President John F. Kennedy, and up through the present instant.

This weakness has been permitted, in large part, because of an often potentially fatal, wrong-headed belief, respecting the nature of imperialism. The Romans were already clear on this distinction within the body of what has been considered as "natural law" for such matters. The power of the emperor was situated, qualitatively, above, and apart from the mere "kings" of the nations subject to the higher authority of actual imperial rule. Today, in modern European and related types of society, it is the dominant financier-monetarist interest which embodies the imperial reign ontologically.

So, disregard for that distinction licenses the practice of a misguided, but widespread belief, the which identifies the notion of "empire" with a simply misguided notion of imperialism as being the simple subordination of one nation, or nations, to another.

On that account, in fact, since the time of the Peloponnesian War, all forms of Europe-centered imperialism, including the case of British imperialism today, have not been the imperialism of a nation, but a monetary imperialism like that expressed in a typical form, today, by the coincidence of the U.S. Nixon Administration's cancellation of the fixed-exchange-rate system, on the one hand, with Lord Jacob Rothschild's 1971 launching of his Inter-Alpha Group, on the other. That latter, Inter-Alpha Group, is, in reality, a single, London-centered Group of assorted gangs, composed, like the Persian horde at the battle of Gaugamela, of a functionally unified assortment which dominates the field of its about-to-be-defeated army: a reported 70-percentile of the financial power of the world, either explicitly, or through the relationship of a keystone to an arch.

This is ancient pattern of Mediterranean-centered imperialism, whose medieval and modern expressions

---

6. Incidentally, they also seem to dislike me personally, very much.

are to be traced from the root of the rise of Venice as a monetary power, to supersede the imperial power of Byzantium, since about 1000 A.D., and from the modern wars already launched by the orchestrations of a revived Venice's efforts to destroy the accomplishments which had been set into motion by the launching of the beginning of modern European civilization by the great ecumenical Council of Florence.

On that subject: the obvious question so posed, is one which should be nothing which differs from: "but, what is the pathogen which spreads the disease?" In fact, imperialism is not an action of a particular nation, but is a disease of more or less pandemic character, as Rosa Luxemburg, and, later, also our State Department's Herbert Feis understood this, and as the case of the extended present reach of Lord Jacob Rothschild's Inter-Alpha Group and its auxiliaries since 1971.

I should emphasize, for the edification of doubters here, that it is not the U.S. government which presently reigns over the global policy-shaping of the U.S.A., but rather what is called "Wall Street." "Wall Street," which, together with the Boston-based "Vault" were launched, directly, from London, as direct creations of British Lord Shelburne's imperial East India Company. This creation has persisted as an imperial force throughout the planet, to the present day, since the February 1763 close of both the Seven Years War in Europe and the parallel "French and Indian Wars" in North America.

See Anton Chaitkin's *Treason in America* (1985) and historian H. Graham Lowry's *How the Nation Was Won* (1988)[7], on the following subject-matters:

The 2008-2010 "bail-out" in the U.S.A. expresses the looting of the United States as a nation, that, presently, since August 1971, into the ground, that on orders from British empire agents such as President George W. Bush, Jr. and, later, outright British puppet and virtual traitor, President Barack Obama. The case of the rape of the United States by British Petroleum, now, is merely an illustration of who is giving imperial orders to whom, and, chiefly, on the behalf of the British empire and its British Petroleum, under what many of our patriots may be coming to consider the treasonous character of the currently incumbent U.S. President.

On that spoken note, our attention is now returned, for a time, to the matter of that infectious mental disease of entire peoples and nations which I have classified as "reductionism as a mental illness."

To simplify the task which I have now set before us in this report, at least somewhat, I refer the reader to my own, recent, March 2010 piece, titled **Mapping the Cosmos.**[8]

The Cosmic View

My reference to this use of that term, "Cosmos," is as minted by Alexander von Humboldt, of *Cosmos* fame, the one time leading figure (and collaborator of France's honored "Author of Victory" Lazare Carnot) within France's Ecole Polytechnique, and, member and associate of that same Ecole. The case of the great science-master von Humboldt expresses my emphasis on the relevant conceptions introduced since the time of the British monarchy's 1890 ouster of Germany's Chancellor Bismarck and to the rising importance of the work of Academician V.I. Vernadsky's mapping of the presently known universe as composed of a set of the three distinct, but interacting categories of the presently known universe, the *lithosphere*, *biosphere*, and *noösphere*.

That latter set is to be contrasted, absolutely, to toleration of the contrary viewpoints bearing any semblance of that Newtonian school echoed by the nonsense of such among Vernadsky's adversaries as the British accomplices of Bertrand Russell, and J.B.S. Haldane, such as the Soviet Union's wretchedly reductionist A.I. Oparin, or similar Russian and other admirers of the tradition of the British empire's International Institute for Applied Systems Analysis (IIASA). British Liberalism is the putrid essence of all modern imperialism since, in fact, that February 1763 Peace of Paris which established Lord Shelburne's British East India Company as the kernel of what became the British Empire of Queen Victoria, her successor, and her monarchy to the present date.

Admittedly, there are important elements of influence in present-day Russia, as elsewhere, which deny any attachment to the presently continued existence of the British Empire as such.[9] Among Russians today, that regrettable belief is often traced to a certain inter-

---

7. *How the Nation Was Won* is availabe at http://store.larouchepub.com/product-p/eirbk-1988-1-0-0-pdf.htm

8. Available in the March 19, 2010 issue of **EIR** at http://www.larouchepub.com/eiw/public/2010/2010_10-19/2010-11/pdf/04-24_3711.pdf

9. A "little England," or modest government composed of the territorial components and population of the United Kingdom, were a desirable alternative to that empire of which that territory is essentially only another among many victims of British imperialism.

Three Categories of Human Thought

The relatively highest category of human thought, is typified by that of such as Pythagoras, Plato, an Archytas, a system of thought based upon the scientific principle of hypothesis, also known as "Socratic thinking."

Pythagoras (ca. 570-495 B.C.)

Archytas (ca. 428-347 B.C.)

Plato (ca. 428-348 B.C.)

The second category is typified by the followers of Aristotle, as the domain of substitution of intrinsically corrupted a priori presumptions, e.g., the corruption expressed by Euclid's denial of the existence of either God's or man's power of genuine creativity within the present universe.

Aristotle (384-322 B.C.)

Euclid (ca. 325-270 B.C.)

national strain of professedly Communist or related pedigree associated with the duped devotees of the British Fabian Society's Frederick Engels, the same Engels who played a signal role in launching the career of British gun-runner and devotee of "permanent warfare, permanent revolution," and of the British Empire, Alexander Helphand.

Since Ancient History

To situate those systemic distinctions within the relevant, broader historical context, we must reflect on those three leading currents of systemic thinking found among the combined Mediterranean littoral and the Near East region, as a region known to us from the ancient through contemporary history of European epistemology since approximately the self-inflicted fall of Sumer, and since the great scientific accomplishment of the erection of the great Pyramid of Giza.

The first of those three categories is typified by what came to be known as socalled Greek civilization's Pythagoreans, and by followers of the Pythagoreans'

method, such as Plato. The second, opposing current, expressed that systemic degeneration of mental behavior associated with Aristotle and Euclid. The third, is that of the modern followers of Paolo Sarpi, that liberal school of European statistical irrationalism expressed as the post-Franklin Roosevelt failed economic policies of both the U.S.A. and European cultural hegemonies of the same period, especially since the wretched changes introduced during the 1968-1981 interval, and, later, since the advent of the malicious Alan Greenspan's entry into the post of Wall Street and London agent, as Federal Reserve Chairman.

The relatively highest category of human thought, as typified by that of such as the Pythagoreans and Plato, is a system of thought based upon the scientific principle of hypothesis. This category is typified by the process of discovery and realization of universal principles which are proven by means of a certain quality of experiment best known to us under such rubrics as "Socratic thinking," or as illustrated by the examples provided by both Pythagoreans, such as that friend of Plato's known as the great Archytas, and by Plato himself. Cardinal Nicholas of Cusa could be, therefore, fairly identified as a modern follower of Plato. The U.S. Declaration of Independence and the Preamble of the U.S. Federal Constitution, are to be read as modern expressions of a renewal of the Platonic principle.

The second category among the three, is typified by

The third is that of the modern European Liberalism of the followers of Paolo Sarpi, typified by the present British ideological system of "liberalism," as one finds in Adam Smith's statistical methods.

Adam Smith
(1723-1790 A.D.)

Paolo Sarpi
(1552-1623 A.D.)

the followers of Aristotle, as the domain of substitution of intrinsically corrupted *a-priori* presumptions for the principle of hypothesis, as the corruption expressed by such as Euclid's denial of the existence of either God's or man's power of genuine creativity within the present universe.

The third, in the order of appearance, is that of the modern European Liberalism of the followers of Paolo Sarpi. That is typified by the present British ideological system of "liberalism," in which there are, avowedly, as Adam Smith put the point, no principles of the type known as being characteristic of the kind of known physical principles specific to the tradition of the Pythagoreans and Plato, but only what is often termed as statistical methods for a merely pragmatic science which, by definition, excludes consideration of actually fundamental principles, as Adam Smith illustrates this case.[10] It is for this reason that all economists of the Liberal persuasion have been consistently incompetent in their efforts at economic forecasting.

The last of the three views, is that which is actually responsible for bringing upon us the great, global economic-breakdown crisis of the post-July 2007 period to date.

However, for long periods of the U.S.A.'s existence

---

10. E.g., *Theory of Moral Sentiments* (1759) and *The Wealth of Nations* (1776).

under its implicitly Platonic Federal Constitution, ever since the Massachusetts Bay colony, for as long as it retained its Royal charter, the long, constitutional trend of U.S. policy has been that of a fixed-exchange-rate system of physical progress per capita and per square kilometer. This latter principle of economy, is specific to the U.S.A., whenever it has been allowed to function under the protection of a fixed-exchange-rate principle, a principle expressed in a return to the philosophical standpoint traced, implicitly, to Plato and what he would recognize as his antecedents.

The principled forerunner of the constitutional American System of political economy, is, thus, to be traced, fairly, to such standards as those of Socrates and Plato, as those are immediately opposed to followers of the Delphi cult of Apollo-Dionysos, such as those associated with its last reigning priest of Delphi in Roman imperial times, Plutarch.

In that sense, the specific quality of that American System of government is, that it truly represents a universal model, since the treaty-agreements natural to that system provide for its extension to serve, potentially, as the virtual keystone of a universal system among what must be, respectively, perfectly sovereign nation-states of varying local constitutional forms of cultures.

For example: the normal treaty-relationship among the present or prospective, sovereign partners of our United States under present and future conditions, is a connection premised upon two general economic principles common to the partners: a.) a shared form of regulation of credit coherent with what President Franklin D. Roosevelt established in 1933, under a Glass-Steagall law governing banking and public credit, and also, b.) with what that same President Roosevelt established, in the global form of a fixed-exchange-rate system, the system set during the July 1-22, 1944, Bretton Woods Conference, to serve as the common instrument among the currencies of the participating nation-state partners.

There is nothing which *should be* mysterious to qualified scholars and scientists respecting the uniqueness of the American model of a system of political-economy. The knowledge on which the development of that American system was premised, was knowledge assembled in a modern European quality and form, through the influence of such leaders of the Fifteenth-century European Renaissance as the initiative of, chiefly, Filippo Brunelleschi and Cardinal Nicholas of

Cusa.

For example, the main branch of the development of modern European physical science, was an expression of the heritage delivered by Brunelleschi and Cusa to such explicit followers of Cusa as Luca Pacioli, and of that Leonardo da Vinci whose most notable, avowed follower in science, was, later, the Johannes Kepler who was the only unique discoverer of the principle of universal gravitation.

Kepler was a key source of the knowledge which prompted the principal physical-scientific achievements of the Gottfried Leibniz who was the one and only original discoverer of the calculus, a calculus based on a specification which Leibniz had adopted from an instruction presented to "future mathematicians" by Kepler, as was the development of the notions of elliptical functions as physical, rather than formal mathematical functions, by the collaborators of Carl F. Gauss.

The essential realization of these cardinal advances from about the time of the great ecumenical Council of Florence, onwards, through the work of Gauss, was launched through the instrument of the justly celebrated 1854 habilitation dissertation of Bernhard Riemann. Noting the crucial role contributed in this fashion, all the main currents of competent modern scientific principle, which exclude reductionists such as the so-called "mathematical physicists," are associated with the emergence of what was to become known as the science of physical chemistry, from the time of such as Louis Pasteur.

Under the terms of the renewal of such treaty-partnerships which had been launched under the leadership of President Franklin Roosevelt, but betrayed through the collusion of President Harry S Truman with British Prime Minister Winston Churchill:

What I have proposed as the immediate action to set such a most urgently needed, new agreement among nations into motion, would be appropriately launched as an agreement on those specifically proposed points of universal agreement which I have projected as being launched by a group of sovereign nation-states inclusive of a core grouping of the United States of America, Russia, China, and India. This would also include those other nations which were prepared to join those four to create an initiating body for the needed reform in affairs among nations generally.

That said so far, there is an underlying principle of action which must be included as an intention, in order to bring the goal of such cooperation into the form of a successful remedy for the presently desperate state of world affairs.

That principle is typified as a Promethean quality of commitment to a relatively capital-intensive progress in the science-driven progress of the productive powers of labor, per capita, and per square kilometer, globally, and perpetually.

Notably, the relatively long term perspective of realizing a reasonably successful round-trip of mankind to and from Mars, after allowing for three successive generations of recovery of mankind from the ruinous effects which the planet considered as a whole has suffered since the assassination of U.S. President John F. Kennedy, which have ruined the productive powers of labor in the trans-Atlantic region of the world to such a degree that the reversal of that ruinous decay over the course of time, means that the development of the mission-oriented schooling of at least two entire generations of the populations of the trans-Atlantic region are probably required to launch the realization of the Promethean goals associated with the initial success of the intention to reach beyond the Moon in a successful manned transit to, and return from Mars.

II. Aeschylus' "Prometheus Bound"

Not unlike many subjects of serious consideration respecting categories of human behavior, the subject of "imperialism" can be approached in two ways: once, by identifying its footprint, a point of view which often does more to confuse, than clarify the issues; second, the ontological content corresponding to *the process of generation* of that subject-matter. The latter is something which no faithful dupe of the evil Paolo Sarpi's Liberalism would wish to understand.

On this subject, we must distinguish what has been merely a form of policy—the virtual footprint, from the actual principle which defines the functional content. In short: *what, in real-life history, is the difference between the mind of the master, and that of the slave of the mere appearances?* What merely appear to be the issues of their time, issues such as the causes for ruinous long wars?

I have spoken and written, on that subject, on a number of earlier occasions over recent years; I restate the point afresh, but from a slightly higher standpoint.

There are myths which lead us to the source of that shadow cast by a less understood, actual substance of the matter. So, Aeschylus' Prometheus Bound performs such a service. (Sculpture by Nicolas-Sébastien Adam, 1762)

First, now, we must identify the specific, chronic state of the world's warfare orchestrated, essentially, by the British Empire, throughout the entire sweep of world history since 1890, and up through the present efforts of that Empire to bring about the final destruction of the United States of America through included assistance from the British puppet-President of our U.S.A., Barack Obama.

The Schumpeter Follies

What was then a new quality in modern warfare has dominated the world since the British monarchy effected the 1890 ouster of Germany's Chancellor Otto von Bismarck. The condition has been chronic through the present time. This is to be traced, in simple fact, as a set of consequences which first appeared in rapid-fire succession with the 1894 assassination of France's President Marie François Sadi Carnot, the Dreyfus Case, and the British Prince of Wales' prompting Ja-

pan's Mikado in launching a virtually permanent state of war against China, Korea, and Russia, all with the continuing, institutional effects[11] through the time of the surrender of Japan to General Douglas MacArthur in August 1945, effects still reverberating throughout the world at large today.

With the death of President Roosevelt on April 12, 1945, and the surrender of the Mikado on September 2, 1945, the 1939-1945 "World War II" itself had more or less come to an end. However; what began, even back then, as the continuing effort for the intended destruction of our U.S.A., by the British Empire, has been continued since the death of President Franklin Roosevelt in a new guise, through to the present day of the reign of the British monarchy's puppet, President Barack Obama.

The post-1890 process of open British imperial intent for warfare against our U.S. republic, has been a reaction which has been associated with the British Prince of Wales Albert Edward's rise in status to what a famous portrait depicted as the fatuous figure of a "Lord of the Isles." So, in this way, the failure of the effort of Jeremy Bentham's trained successor at the British Foreign Office, Lord Palmerston, to employ its puppet, the London-created Confederacy, to crush the United States out of existence, was combined, in effect, with the consolidation of the continental United States and the great agro-industrial revolution launched under President Abraham Lincoln. Lincoln's leadership to this effect, during his lifetime, had resulted in the echoes of that American triumph of statecraft which was echoed within continental Eurasia by the response of the revolutionary industrial revolution launched by both Germany's Bismarck and Russia's Dmitri Mendeleyev, all in response to the evidence of grand, worldwide achievements radiating from the 1876 Philadelphia Centennial Exposition.

Imperial Britain's enraged reaction to these American developments and their echoes in continental Europe, was expressed by a series of crucial, triggering events leading into the so-called First World War, events beginning the ouster of Bismarck; but, the most crucial of all was the use of a European terrorist imported into Manhattan with the intent of assassinating U.S. President William McKinley.

---

11. With lasting effects on the U.S.A.'s Presidency itself until the 1933 inauguration of President Franklin D. Roosevelt, of the assassination of U.S. President William McKinley in 1901.

The virtually dynastic change from President McKinley to Confederacy fellow-travellers Presidents Theodore Roosevelt and Ku Klux Klan fanatic Woodrow Wilson, was the passing of the Presidency from a patriot to a child of the British-created Confederacy which set the stage for the British Empire's preparations for and launching of what became known as "World War II." The immediate consequence of that assassination of President McKinley was the moving the United States from an opponent of Britain's launching of what became known as "World War I," which it had been under McKinley, to an ally of the British imperial cause. That arrangement continued until a clear-headed patriot, Franklin D. Roosevelt, assumed the Presidency and brought a Britain almost crushed by its own folly in creating and launching the Adolf Hitler tyranny, begging for rescue at the knees of Franklin Roosevelt.

Then, with the death of President Franklin Roosevelt, the British gang aligned with Wall Street asset Harry S Truman, returned to refresh what had been the dubious intentions of British puppets Theodore Roosevelt, Woodrow Wilson, and U.S. President Calvin Coolidge.

Examining this aspect of U.S. history in a finer detailing of the causes of such ironical turns in the history of those times, the Boston State Street and New York Wall Street financier consort and their British East India Company-spawned political minions, were then, as under President Obama today, the extension of the British empire's financial grip on the economy and those many bought-and-paid-for, leading U.S. politicians who have acted as the minions, as inside the U.S. Congress and other relevant places of political and educational expresses of the British empire of today, politicians who have betrayed their oath of office and the safety of the republic which they had been consigned to serve.

Thus, it came to be the case, that at the present moment, the United States itself is already in the grip of what has been essentially the British empire's orchestration of what that empire intends should be the early economic collapse, and an early end of the United States as a nation. Of late, the British imperialists have been wont to brag brazenly of this intention within the U.S. itself, as through the mouth of an official minion of visiting British Prime Minister David Cameron. Should President Obama be permitted to hold the office of President over the course of the Summer until a point proximate to this coming October, it were probable that

White House/Pete Souza

Obama is a case of what is known, in relevant technical terms, as "a failed personality." He must be tossed out of the Presidency, by proper means, Richard M. Nixon-style.

the United States would have been successfully virtually destroyed, as the British government has hoped, by aid of its accomplice, the Obama Presidency.

This does not signify that that collapse were inevitable. At any instant the 1933 Glass-Steagall law were re-enacted, a sudden turn to a vigorous recovery of the U.S.A.'s economy would be under way. This could not happen without putting President Obama into a condition of virtual retirement from office during the course of these present Summer months. Allowing him to continue to rule through a time as early as the November 2010 Federal election, would virtually guarantee the extinction of the U.S.A. as a republic. Obama's very continuation in office is now fairly estimated as virtually treasonous by the measure of the existing and clearly foreseeable, relevant effects.

Therefore, that Obama must be ousted before the Summer has ended, perhaps even earlier. There is, incidentally, no lack of the available evidence of suitable cause required to lawfully effect his ouster. It is to be emphasized that Obama is another case of what is termed in relevant technical terms, as "a failed personality," that in the clinical likeness of the Emperor Nero and Adolf Hitler, the likeness of a pair of failed personalities which had ended their incumbency in power with suicide. Obama must not be permitted to carry out the potential commitment to suicide embedded within his defective personality, but he must be tossed out of the Presidency by proper means, Richard M. Nixon-style.

U.S. President Dwight D. Eisenhower, with whom I exchanged very brief, but relevant correspondence in 1947, explicitly encouraged my outlook for his prospective Presidential candidacy against "that little man," Harry S Truman, then, but deferred his candidacy to what might be a more appropriate time. By the time that General Eisenhower sought and gained the nomination for President, the leading political situation inside the U.S.A. had been changed for the worse.

Eisenhower had become the legend of what was sometimes seen as "Eisenhowever" in his time as President. His former Columbia University colleague, and den-mother of what came to be widely known as Milton Friedman, Arthur Burns, proved to be an economic catastrophe in his own right. Nonetheless; on crucial strategic issues, President Eisenhower sometimes played a very necessary, crucial, and commanding role in the history of that decade, and still later as a former President. As it turned out, Eisenhower's successor, President John F. Kennedy acted as a patriot with genuine accomplishments, until a set of imported assassins cleared the way for that foolish Indo-China war which was intended, by the then living heirs of Lord Shelburne's 1782 creation of the British Foreign Office, all chiefly to the intent to ruin the political and economic institutions of our United States.

So, the subsequent Presidencies of those virtual puppet-Presidents Richard Nixon, Jimmy Carter, George H.W. Bush, George W. Bush, Jr., and, presently, Barack Obama, have virtually transported the United States to the yawning gates of Hell under Obama today.

The long wars, beginning with the so-called "Cold War," and the chronic warfare in Africa and Asia, and the new Balkan wars, have been cast in the image of the satanic influence of Friedrich Nietzsche, an influence which assumed the inherited name of the Schumpeter dogma, that Fabian disease known as what is to be described clinically as the "Nietzschean" doctrine of "creative destruction," a doctrine, associated with the name of Schumpeter, which remains notorious for such among the effects of its application by British Prime Minister Harold Wilson which, by ruining the economy of the United Kingdom, curiously paved the way for the systemic ruin of Europe and the United States during and since Wilson's time in office: syphilis is also said to be contagious.

Nations have often engaged in even long, ruinous wars, because of the influence of crippling features of popular habits which affect many persons, through the influence of erroneous habits of "blind faith in sense-certainty." So, wars such as a silly U.S.A.'s plunge into ruinous wars, still today, such as the U.S.A. Indo-China War, the repeated wars against Iraq, and the presently continuing, monstrously foolish long war in defense of British drug-trafficking, in Afghanistan, may be located in the failure to recognize that what are taken for the senses innate to our biological organization, are, contrary to popular belief, what were appropriately identified, symbolically, as merely "meter readings." Consequently, in and of themselves, these readings may be accurate in some fashion, (if only as meter-readings, of course), but they do not represent the matter of the actual "real universe" which those readings might have seem to have reflected.

Wars of the type which have become more or less chronic, especially worse than useless long wars, since the U.S. Truman Administration, must be recognized as being a leading part of a repertoire of the rampant plague of Schumpeteran destruction spread throughout most of the planet now.

There is a deeper, truly Satanic, Nietzschean, existentialist, motive behind it all. To understand how Satan works to such effect, we must probe deeply into the human soul, its native virtues and its often corrupted incarnations.

Irony as Scientific Truth

As our already referenced William Empson had emphasized for the case of Classical artistic composition, in his *Seven Types of Ambiguity*, the reality "behind the meter-readings," is locatable by us, but only through the agency of *that principle of metaphor* which is the essential component of all actually Classical artistic composition, such as that of J.S. Bach, Wolfgang Mozart, and Ludwig Beethoven for music, as for William Shakespeare, Gotthold Lessing, Friedrich Schiller, and Percy Bysshe Shelley for poetry and drama, and, similarly, as for all of the true principles of true discovery of universal principles, such as the discovery of gravitation by Johannes Kepler, which have been the true accomplishments of the work of physical science.

So, this notion of metaphor, as emphasized by Empson, is the subject-matter which is encountered in the foundations of modern physical science, as in the case of such expressions as the great scientist Johannes Kepler's uniquely original discovery of the principle of universal gravitation, as being recognized as the physically lawful expression of the ironical (or, metaphorical) juxtaposition of sight and harmonics. As in Kepler's uniquely original discovery of the principle of gravitation, neither sight, nor harmonics, when either were taken by itself, is "the truth" of our experience of the universe; the truth lies in that kind of unique, ironical conjunction of the two, which is expressed by the noëtic principle of Classical artistic composition, as for the case treated by Empson.

As I have emphasized, repeatedly, in major writings during the recent two years, we have the following subject to consider on this account.

In an accurate estimate of our experience from inside the experience of the individual human life of any truly great scientist since the Pythagoreans and Plato, we travel in time through the physical space-time of experience, as in the manner of a pilot operating from within a capsule which affords him no direct sensory experience of the physical space-time through which he is traveling, In such a case, each among us must rely on an insightful reading of what must seem to be a special kind of mutually contradictory meter-readings, such as what are called "sense impressions." Such experience of sense-impressions typifies the predicament posed to the awareness of any competent scientist, such as the cases of the modern Max Planck and Albert Einstein, or, earlier, such wonderful discoveries of universal truth as in the known work of the ancient Archytas,[12] Plato, or Eratosthenes.[13]

So it is, in all cases of a scientifically competent reading of the meaning expressed to kindred effects by crucial juxtapositions giving arise to true, intrinsically anti-entropic notions of universal principle in our experience of the universe. Here we meet the principle of metaphor, as expressed by William Empson in the argument which Empson adopts from such arguments as those of Percy Bysshe Shelley's *A Defence of Poetry*, and which also, in fact, echoes Johannes Kepler's earlier, uniquely original discovery of the inherently anti-entropic principle of universal gravitation.

Now, from the case of our pilot traveling in physical space-time, proceed as follows:

There is a certain story, told in certain circles, which,

while not exactly the true story, is a myth which leads us to the source of that shadow cast by a less understood, actual substance of the matter. So, Aeschylus' *Prometheus Bound* performs such a service. Such are matters consistent with both the hypothetical case of the space-pilot, above, and the role of the notion of *metaphor* presented in the argument of (in particular) William Empson's *Seven Types of Ambiguity*. Such are the subject-matters featured within this present chapter.

Thus, to begin this present chapter, I have referred, again, to my original encounter with that work by Empson. I have since learned, since that fresh encounter, that the emphasis required in reading Empson's work is that which I have placed on the equivalence of his notion of metaphor, to that of Johannes Kepler's uniquely original discovery of the principle of gravitation, as in his *Harmonies of the World*. Thus, Empson, in particular, had returned to the Classical notions of such as William Shakespeare, rather than the Sarpian, Liberal romanticism of Shakespeare-hater Sir Francis Bacon.[14]

The understanding of those functional distinctions which separate British empiricist ideology, and its likenesses, from both science and sanity, is to be attained through rising above those misleading notions of so-called "sense-certainty" which exert a virtual dictatorship over virtually all so-called "sovereign" peoples today.[15]

---

12. E.g., Archytas' uniquely original duplication of the cube.

13. Eratosthenes' discovery of the size of the Earth through instrument readings crafted within a north-south positioning, in Syene and Alexandria, of observations of the Sun within a region of ancient Egypt.

14. To understand Empson's argument, it were useful to look to the treatment of Shakespeare by the circles of Abraham Kästner, including such followers of Kästner as Gotthold Lessing, Moses Mendelssohn, and the circles of Friedrich Schiller. My ontological definition of human creativity is the key to understanding the underlying issues of such matters. It is the cult of so-called "mathematical physics," as established to wide effect, since 1716, through the influence of Abbé Antonio S. Conti's direction, which excluded the creative powers of the mind, which lie within the domain of Classical modes of artistic creation, and do not exist as actually universal principles under the reign of a so-called "mathematical physics" of such as, for example, a personally decent David Hilbert or a consummately despicable Bertrand Russell.

15. It is important, at this point in the present chapter, to place emphasis on the strict use of the English term "empiricism." It signifies that doctrine of Paolo Sarpi which is presented as the dogma of British Liberalism ("empiricism") which is the central principle of economy for Adam Smith, as in Smith's 1759 *Theory of Moral Sentiments*: "Nature has directed us to the greater part of these by original and immediate instincts. Hunger, thirst, the passion which unites the two sexes, the love of pleasure, and the dread of pain, prompt us to apply these means for their own sakes, and without any consideration of their tendency to those beneficent ends which the great Director of nature intended to produce by them." Hence, in empiricism, the statistical apprehension of pleasure and pain define the entire method of a notion of the principles

This fact is, what is typified as the basis for my own long-standing campaign against that delusion which I have known, with increasing precision as to principle, to be the sheer, Sarpian fraud of the pathetic belief in any teaching of physics which is subsumed by mere mathematics. I have frequently referred to such cases as, on the one hand, that of David Hilbert, or, on the other, the sheer evil represented by the devotees of Bertrand Russell and the cult of the International Institute for Applied Systems Analysis (IIASA). This is a matter more readily understood from the vantage-point presented in the course of this present chapter. It is crucial-experimental qualities of physical principles which must determine the mathematical procedures in scientific practice, principles which are contrary to the same cult of Sarpi's Liberalism which IIASA reflects, rather than the other way around.

Such are the terms in which the causes for the follies of ruinous long wars may be sought.

I will resume the development of that argument, after the following intermediate historical references.

Plato vs. Aristotle & Sarpi

Therefore, it is most notable, that what have been most widely accepted as standards of popular culture among European cultures, in particular, are, first, the fraudulent epistemological legacy of the ancient Aristotle, and, second, that modern cult of Paolo Sarpi which was launched to become what is to be recognized as the modern European, Venetian-designed, monetarist cult of British Liberalism. In both of those cases, the existence of a principle of human creativity is not only denied, but fiercely hated, hated in what must be recognized as being an actually Satanic passion typified by opinions such as those of Paolo Sarpi himself, his "Leporello," Galileo, Rene Descartes, and the Abbé Antonio S. Conti who crafted the notorious French disease known as "Voltaire" out of a certain substance.

Therefore, we have the slight, but nonetheless systemic contrast, between an Aristotle who presumes *a-priori* "zero growth" presumptions, whereas Paolo Sarpi denies that any actual knowledge of the organiza-

tion of experience is accessible to the knowledge of human individuals, as Adam Smith echoed Sarpi in Smith's own 1759 *Theory of Moral Sentiments*.

Thus, it is with Abbé Antonio S. Conti's launching of what became the widespread hoax of the Anglo-Dutch Liberals' cult which produced Sir Isaac Newton, a hoax launched on a broad scale by Abbé Conti, that globally extended European civilization has been dominated, although not entirely, by a conflict among three mutually contradictory systems of thinking concerning scientific and political matters:[16] first, the sanity typified by Plato, second, the fraud by Aristotle, and, third, the filthy insanity spread Liberally by Sarpi and his dupes.

The most obvious indication of the earliest of those three contending systems, is typified by the contrast of the case of the Pythagoreans and Plato, when contrasted with the cases of the Aristotelean and Sarpian systems of opinion. The case for the Pythagoreans and Plato, is known to us presently as some ancient mariners' culture's discovery of some knowable physical principle of astronomy, as used, for example, for transoceanic navigation, the first true notion of an implicitly finite, ordered array, the true universal principle which replaced the mere, naive admiration, as with a gaping mouth, of the stellar array.

The case presented by the work of such as the Pythagoreans and Plato, was a discovery which must have begun to be understood no later than during the last great period of glaciation in the world's northern maritime regions. It was defined among the great ancient navigators long before the use of the name of geodesy, that the idea of an actual notion of the existence of universal scientific principles was expressed in adducible cases of actual practice, such as the practice of Sphaerics and the work of the maritime culture of the Pythagoreans such as the celebrated Archytas. Only a trans-oceanic maritime culture could have developed what Plato came to know, through recognizing the stellar universe as expressing a single physical principle of a "finite but unbounded" universe, as one of the three principal periods within the Earth orbit itself.

The wretched devotee of the Delphi cult, Aristotle, copying the doctrine of the Olympian Zeus which had been condemned in Aeschylus' *Prometheus* Trilogy,

---

of an economy. Thus, all my notable opponents among economic forecasters have consistently failed throughout the entire 1956-2010 interval during which I have made forecasts (rather than those manifestly silly opinions called "statistical predictions").

---

16. Notably, since Conti had received the news confirming Gottfried Leibniz's death.

had forbidden both God and man, alike, from participating in any act of actual creativity, once the universe had reached the point of development in time that it had been established, in Aristotle's view, as a kind of mindless clockwork. In contrast to Aristotle's system, Sarpi's Liberalism, simply denied human beings any knowledge of the actual principles of either man or nature. The mathematical systems of Aristotle (e.g., Euclid) and the utterly depraved Sarpi, were represented in their worst outcome by such wretched creatures as Bertrand Russell and his devotees of the International Institute for Applied Systems Analysis (IIASA). The Russell schemes represent the extremes of the depravity which must be regarded as appropriate causes for the entire planet's presently onrushing general economic breakdown-crisis.

Against that background, now consider the view which I share with Plato, among others.

NASA

'The Universe as Our Ocean': The only presently conceivable basis for a known history of civilization, has been the discovery of the role of the stellar night-time array as a navigational map of a Keplerian, finite, but boundless universe of reliable oceanic navigation, over long intervals of the history of what have been essentially maritime cultures.

The Universe as Our Ocean

The only presently conceivable basis for a known history of civilization, for better or worse, has been the discovery of the role of the stellar night-time array as a navigational map of a Keplerian, finite, but boundless universe of reliable oceanic navigation, that over persisting long intervals of the history of what have been essentially maritime cultures.

As I have emphasized this same point, directly, or implicitly, in various locations, the advancement of mankind's condition proceeded from such relatively restricted bounds as Mediterranean- and Indian Ocean-based maritime cultures, to the improvement brought about by riparian cultures internal to systems of combined rivers and canals, to the still higher order of trans-oceanic cultures spread from the Mediterranean, to the superseding of internal water-borne systems by the dominant functions of trans-continental rails in non-decadent European and other cultures presently. This much so far, presages an intra-Solar system, manned exploration, and human settlement.

Presently, the progress of civilization into the domain of interplanetary human activity, has been hampered by what are such relatively morally obvious deficiencies as the problem of failing to solve the challenge of problems of gravitation and related issues of cosmic radiation which confront us most obviously when we send human beings, rather than mere robotic equipment into interplanetary space. Yet, already, human interplanetary space-travel, and the prospect of related habitation, tend more to haunt us, than to afford us a satisfactory feeling for this reality. That lack of a satisfactory "feeling" in respect to such matters, is among my concerns in this report: to understand war, we must acquire a confident insight into the higher realities of the relevant kinds of follies in history.[17]

Thus, as I have emphasized in an earlier publication, the prospect of human exploration of nearby Solar space, already haunts us with the need for a fresh definition of the term "basic economic infrastructure." The

---

17. This is a very crucial point to be emphasized here in the concluding portion of this present report.

challenge is relatively new in the annals of contemporary awareness, but the challenge has already been there since the earliest successes in trans-oceanic navigation.

"Infrastructure" does not merely signify a supplementing of the development of production and communication; it represents the developing foundation on which the progress of the power of production depends: the development of the powers of production are dependent upon the advances in technology in infrastructure. I mean this in the specific sense that I have pointed to the role of the discovery of the starry universe as the representation of a conceptually finite universe, as being the universe of a society whose existence is based on transoceanic navigation—a true maritime system. Or since the addition of a riparian system of rivers and canals, or the development of a transcontinental railway system as transcending an existing riparian system, and, since, still later, the case of successively more advanced systems of powering the forces of a continent, and, then, presently, a system dependent upon the development of the global application of nuclear-fission and thermonuclear power.

I mean to emphasize, by that statement, that the continued existence of civilized society demands the persistent increase of the relative energy-flux-density in the modes of power employed, and also in the capital-intensity of the organization of not only production, but the very means of continued existence of a society's culture.

So, the possibility of the advances in productive technology and productive powers of labor premised on the use of coal and petroleum for the increase of industrial power per capita and per square kilometer, illustrates the point most simply and clearly. Today, the ability to sustain the general human population depends absolutely on accelerated development of nuclear-fission and nuclear-fusion power, as superseding what are presently policies of foolish reliance on such moronic, low energy-flux densities as the modalities of "solar" and "wind" power.

The most crucial of the determining considerations bearing upon physical productivity of a society, per capita and per square kilometer of territory, is what I have already referenced here as the principle of Leibnizian dynamics expressed, typically, in the physical concept of "applied energy-flux density." This is measurable, in one aspect, as applicable power expressed per square-centimeter of cross-section of the flow of power. This means power usable by mankind at the lowest level of the incidence of sunlight at the Earth's surface, or wind-power, up through the use of increasingly "hot" forms of fuels, up through generated electrical power at high densities, and into nuclear and thermonuclear processes as fuels.

Thus, it is urgent that we not use solar-radiation sources or wind directly, not only because such primitive fuels are inefficient, but because the only decent general use of sunlight as a fuel is its role expressed through such natural means as the chlorophyll principle. Every dollar wasted on solar cells used for a substitute fuel, is an area which is condemned to be a wasteland by stealing from the magnificent benefits of chlorophyll in effecting a great improvement in the entire cycle from sunlight, through chlorophyll, as fruitful supplies of the biological processes which make land habitable.

The modern adoption of the ancient Delphic cult of Dionysus, which is what the entirety of the so-called "green movement" of today represents, is a specifically anti-human cult, typified by the implicitly satanic cult of Friedrich Nietzsche and the devotees of Schumpeter's folly.

At its pinnacle, the development of higher forms of sources of power, as typified by nuclear-fission and thermonuclear-fusion sources, defines the possibility of advancement of the power of mankind to exist, not only on Earth, but within the future developments within the Solar system and galaxy beyond. The same principle is expressed as the general level of applied energy-flux density to the productivity of agriculture, manufacturing and general infrastructure of society's population. In fact, every relevant advance in technology reflects this, as in the expression of physical capital-intensity and the level of advancement of the culture of the population.

These considerations define what can be properly assessed as the level of productivity achieved by the advancement, in terms of capital-intensity and energy-flux density, of the social process as a whole. All competent assessments of relative productivity and of rates of advancement or decline of a national economy must be traced to the underlying factors of increasing physical (as distinguished from merely monetary) capital-intensity and relative increases in energy-flux density expressed in the form of applicable power or scientific and related advances in energy-flux density in both production and the basic economic infrastructure on which any form of economy implicitly depends.

Any contrary opinion on the subject of economics is counterproductive mumbo-jumbo of the type currently peddled from London, Wall Street, and the Obama White House.

On precisely that account, we have now reached the initial, exploratory stages of man's prospect for the stellar objectives represented by the development of the still higher quality of infrastructure needed for mankind's growing role in interplanetary space.

This set of considerations, which requires us to look forward, also obliges us to look backward, to the often overlooked implications which we had failed to understand adequately during the course of our travels toward progress. That said, now consider the true implications of the conception of *physical space-time*, rather than the fallacious notion of *physical-space in time*.

Our Physical Space-Time

As I have just summarized this point, the ability of the world's societies to supply the impetus for the needed raising of the standard of living of the present level of population, even without considering the unavoidable increase of the population associated with such progress, depends upon an increase of power, per capita and per square kilometer, a power measured in terms of qualitative increases in effective energy-flux density of the sources of power applied.

That requirement points toward the inherent challenge of a present transition from an apparently, present, upper limit for sources of required power, from a nuclear-fission mode, to a thermonuclear-fusion mode. The mere existence of that present challenge in progress, respecting the requirements of the planet as a whole, implies the transition from man bounded by the conditions of the relative surface of the Earth, into the domain of mankind's exertion of a functionally relevant control over nearby Solar space. Mankind's true destiny would bring our species into the realm of the stars.

The mere contemplation of the realization of a response to this challenge of progress, signifies, that as mankind begins to move into prospective habitats beyond the protected environment of our planet's surface, that a radically new notion of "infrastructure" has overtaken us.

We must think in terms of "synthetic environments" of a type which provide the "protection" of something equivalent to today's habitual notion of habitable "environment," within Solar and other domains which are "naturally" unsuited to human habitation.

For persons who are seriously qualified to discuss such matters, this notion is accessible as a matter of principle today, even at a time when we have not gained an intellectual mastery of particular such cases. For such thinkers, it is not beyond intellectual reach, to estimate the rates of productivity and increase of "energy-flux density" even to begin to consider a pilot habitation on Mars. It also requires a rapid succession of scientific revolutions in the turn to a "periodic table" of the singularities of cosmic radiation, rather than one still stuck in the tradition of particles. What this means, otherwise, is a shift in man's self-image which lifts the human mind out of the muck of naive sense-certainty, as this is implied by both the discovery of universal gravitation by Kepler and William Empson's concept of the efficiency of that physical principle of metaphor which was already clearly presented by the discoveries of such as Kepler, Leibniz, Riemann, and V.I. Vernadsky.

The Matter of Infrastructure

As I have emphasized this point in locations published earlier, the function of "infrastructure" is not that of a supplement to production. It is the building up, to qualitatively higher levels of the equivalent of "energy-flux density," of the creation of the physical and related foundations on which the establishment and maintenance of a certain quality of range of direct productivity, as per capita, and as per square kilometer, is dependent.

For example, it were impossible to continue to maintain the present level of development of the world's current population upon "solar" and "wind" power. As the challenge of maintaining the current population of Asia and Africa demands, without a "platform" of nuclear and higher energy-flux density embedded in the infrastructure of a society (and, also, the world at large), even the present levels of world population are in jeopardy. Thus, the proper emphasis on accelerated development of nuclear-fission and related high-energy-flux-density sources of generally available power, per square kilometer and per-capita, without which the existing levels of population in the principal nations of Asia were not feasible.

Earlier, the steps of progress were represented by maritime culure, then riparian systems which brought

Army Corps of Engineers

The function of "infrastructure" is the building up, to qualitatively higher levels of "energy-flux density"—the creation of the physical and related foundations on which the establishment and maintenance of a certain quality of range of direct productivity, as per capita, and as per square kilometer, is dependent. Shown: construction on the Dalles Dam, Oregon, completed 1991.

the productive powers of labor to a higher level than mere maritime systems, then the complementing of riparian "platforms" of general productivity which depended absolutely on transcontinental railways, and, now, maglev development of transit systems for people and freight (rather than the highly inefficient long-range trucking as a substitute for rail). The development of generally upgraded water systems, as typified by the case of the well-defined NAWAPA design, would mean a qualitative leap in the productive powers of labor and the quality of the environment for human work and habitation.

In a similar vein, the exploration of nearby planetary space, or inter-spatial locations, requires reaching the higher levels of energy-flux density needed by the specific kinds of artificial environment which are indispensable for the successful adaptation of Earth-like habitation by both human and plant life in such new, exceptional regions for exploration and later habitation. The problems of "low" gravitation on the Moon, or Mars, or in orbiting stations above Earth, are only an advanced sampling of the needed future systems which would require sources of power, as measured in energy-flux density, far beyond anything yet considered as presently practicable. Man within the Solar System, or inhabiting our galaxy, is the challenge which we

must muster the capability of achieving over the course of both the present century and, much more, beyond.

My presently relevant estimate begins with recognition of the systemic destruction, over the interval in the U.S.A. and Europe since the assassination of President John F. Kennedy and the great cultural attrition of the remainder of the 1960s, and the three subsequent decades of decadence, of the productive powers of labor per capita and per square kilometer, within North America and western and central Europe. The intellectual powers of the adolescent generations and young-adult generations, have fallen much lower than that of the U.S. and European labor-force of the 1960s and 1970s.

We will require two generations of vigorous investment in a properly defined meaning of the term "basic economic, social infrastructure," to make up for the lost intellectual and related powers which the current adolescent and early-twenties' young-adult population has suffered. We will require the aggressive reversal of the cultural decline of locations such as North America and Europe under the "green" cultural pandemic's collapse of the development of the young human mind of the post-1968 generations. It would be a quarter-century before the social and intellectual effects of this decadence of the recent thirty years have been suitably repaired, that we might be enabled to effect a net reversal of the vast and deep cultural damage to the post-1968 populations since the "Vietnam War" years sufficiently to presume that we have a general population which could be broadly capable of the qualities and rates of progress which were still possible until the culturally depressive effects of the "Nixon" and "Carter" eras had sunk in.

Nonetheless, despite such difficulties, a minority of our broadly defined employment-age population will be available to prepare the way for the explosion of great scientific and related cultural leaps which we must commit ourselves to bring about during the coming fifty to seventy years immediately before us now.

The social aspects of such a prospective program for the remainder of the present century, will be defined by an emphasis on the kinds of great infrastructure projects which where typified by the Tennessee Valley and Manhattan projects of the Franklin Roosevelt era. We were obliged to "build down," rather than the contrary emphasis on agricultural and industrial progress in production up through the late 1960s. Our industry and infrastructure have been destroyed as if by a Golem gone amok, especially since about 1968. We will be obliged, if we are sane, to emphasize massive U.S. Federal programs of revolutionary emphasis on basic economic infrastructure, such as the urgently needed, and readily awaiting NAWAPA project, a project already designed for the purpose of getting to work on a large scale. The role of the automobile will be curtailed to relatively short range daily, or occasional use, while a new system of high-speed modern rail and magnetic levitation takes over. The great infrastructure programs, such as those, will create the "demand" which drives the market for agricultural and industrial production. The sudden and strict enforcement of a Glass-Steagall law, will, doubtless, wipe out most of the high-binder Wall Street and State Street categories, while regional mercantile banks acting on the basis of wiping out both the U.S. government's and related obligations for support of the financial swinders, will enable the flood of Federal credit needed to fund both the development of the great infrastructure programs and the farming and agriculture which benefit from the credit-driven market for their stimulus of net production of goods and essential services.

With such a sudden and sweeping change in policy, back to the policies which enabled our United States to astonish the world, as at the 1876 Centennial fair, we will depart the present pit of despair. We shall not be suddenly rich, but we shall live productively and with a sense of freedom and restored sense of security, away from the graveyard of lost hopes which the overwhelming majority of our citizenry suffers presently.

It is on the basis of the reform based on both Glass-Steagall and a return to a fixed-exchange-rate system of credit among willing nations, that we shall move toward the great achievements which we shall prepare to realize during the latter half of this present century.

Under such a program, we shall be enabled to free ourselves from the periods of long wars introduced on a global scale by the British Prince of Wales Albert Edward.

III. Necessary, or Bad Wars?

There are no actually "good wars," but there have been some "necessary wars," of which the U.S.A.'s role in so-called "World War II," is an example, or our American Revolution against an Imperial British tyranny. There are also "bad wars." The "baddest" of bad wars, as since the model of the Peloponnesian War, are those, like the U.S. long war in Indo-China, or the wars fought under the Bush family's U.S. Presidencies, or under the worst fool of them all, Barack Obama, in which monetarist power uses wars fomented among the credulous, as the customary way for both creating, and building up a certain kind of imperial power.

Such latter cases are typified by a war set within the ruin of what have been, usually, those long wars, by which a foolishly credulous, and negligent people had brought the tyranny of a monetarist imperial power upon themselves. Such a latter fate was the folly of the duped continental European victims of the newly founded British Foreign Office, those, now duped, former European allies of the American Revolution, whose earlier support for a just war had made possible our victory over the British tyrant, at Yorktown.

With the ouster of Germany's Prince Otto von Bismarck, in 1890, that "bad war" on a global scale, which was identified as the first "world war," was unleashed through a series of the combination of wars, such as the Anglo-Japan warfare launched jointly against China, Korea, and Russia, beginning 1894-1907, and the assassinations of prominent figures, such as, most notably, U.S. President William McKinley, in 1901. This epidemic of folly erupted as in the exemplary assassination of France's President Sadi Carnot, and could not have developed into the outbreak of August 1914, but for that 1901 assasination of U.S. President McKinley which had brought to power a virtual traitor in the Confederacy's tradition, President Theodore Roosevelt.

So, earlier, the French revolution of 1789 and beyond, had turned out to be a bad war which had been orchestrated, beginning the 1782 founding of the British Foreign Office under the Lord Shelburne whose Jeremy Bentham had led the Special Committee of assassinations, wars, and insurrections, which culminated in the destruction of continental Europe, including France itself, by the hand of an unwitting British

While there are no "good wars," there have been necessary wars—for example, the U.S. role in World War II, to defeat the Nazi menace. Shown: the invasion of Normandy; landing ships drop cargo ashore on Omaha Beach, June 1944.

puppet and fully witting, thieving predator, Napoleon Bonaparte.

That much said on this matter so far, look back, stepwise, to the Peloponnesian War.

Some Economists Were Foolish

Begin this study with an examination, from this point onwards, of the most crucial among the functional developments leading into, and beyond what was to become known as "World War I."

Consider one of the more notable symptoms of the folly which permitted the slide into what became not only so-called "World War I," but, also, "World War II," and, then, the long "Cold War." Such was the root of the new phase of global mass-insanity run amok throughout the world since the time that Britain's Margaret Thatcher, flanked by France's culpable President François Mitterrand, and by the failed personality, U.S. President George H.W. Bush had joined forces for the destruction of continental Europe. This trio's culpable actions, had already foredoomed that continent of Europe to the creation of the presently, catastrophically failed, "Euro" system.

Out of a reality which has always remained as con-

trary to the silly notion of "imperialism" adopted by V.I. Lenin, sundry German Social-Democrats, and others, during the run-up to so-called "World War I," and also "World War II," the developments of those two wars, and their aftermath, still today, have proceeded as an expression of the delusion, that imperialism was a phenomenon defined by the role of the individual will and interest of the respective sovereign nation-state. After the sundry, allegedly "world wars" and their like, to date thus far, there arose the even more lunatic misconception, to the effect of proposing some form of "world government" as an imagined remedy for the alleged rapacity, which were alleged to be the fatal flaw embedded in the conception of the sovereign nation-state.

It is important, for the sake of insight into certain crucial realities of the history of modern imperialism and the wars which that imperialist lust has engendered, to recognize that the imperialist orgy of the recent centuries' British monarchy, was not inherent in the United Kingdom's population itself, but, rather, that Kingdom's role as the chief among the puppets of modern Venice, to the present day.

Anyone who has some degree of familiarity with the actual population of the subjects of the United Kingdom itself, must have noticed that many prominent and other figures from that nation, have impulses which our better-informed American patriots would consider as perhaps a bit quaint, but which are, despite that fact, within the bounds of sometimes very useful views of humanity, views we might regard as relatively satisfactory morally. It is not the body of subjects of the United Kingdom, which is the source of the problem of a virtually world-wide British imperialism today. *The empire itself is not that kingdom as such, but a vulturous empire per se, a creature of the Venetian tradition.*

To understand this distinction between nation and

sovereign nation-state, which Lenin, for example, with his notions of principles of economy, never actually understood, we must recognize the curious legacy which must be traced explicitly to the exemplary case of that bloody lunatic known as England's Henry VIII.

With the defeat of Richard III, the constitution of England under Henry VII, had been established as an echo of the great political revolution in France accomplished by King Louis XI, and, implicitly, the radiated impact of the A.D. 1439 Council of Florence. The accomplishment of Louis XI being a revolution premised on the inspiration of Jeanne d'Arc, and upon the same principles as those of the great ecumenical Council of Florence.

The principles expressed by that Council, were reflections of a wide agreement shared with the influence of Cardinal Nicholas of Cusa. Cusa's greatest influence as theologian, statesman, and leading scientist, followed such notable precedents in the development of what became a modern physical science which are typified by the crafting of the cupola of the cathedral of Florence's *Santa Maria del Fiore*, and the *Pazzi Chapel*, by the discoverer of the practical catenary principle, Filippo Brunelleschi.

On the subject of the exemplary British Empire which has now dominated the planet through most of the period since the February 1763 Peace of Paris, until the present time, the following matter of great relevance to the present world crisis, must be said, as preparation, here and now, on the subject of the British empire as such.

What happened, under the regime of what may be defined clinically as the expression of a typical "failed personality," Henry VIII, has been, from that time, until today, the recent British empire's adoption of a kind of reigning, failed personality who often shares a type of mental sickness which that pathetic creature known as today's U.S. President Obama shares, in turn, with famous cases of failed personalities such as that of the Emperor Nero and Adolf Hitler.

President Obama's moral sickness, in particular, expresses the same species of moral-intellectual defect specific to Henry VIII, if, perhaps, not in the matter of wives. The President's mental disorder is an echo of that which was exploited by Venetian interests including King Henry VIII's sexual counselor, and also the Venetian intelligence services' chief Francesco Zorzi (aka "Giorgi"), including, also, Venetian agent and Plantagenet Pretender Cardinal Pole, and other Venetian-owned conspirators, such as the monstrous Thomas Cromwell. That Venetian cabal was used to control the puppet-like king, Henry VIII, by using the king's certain homicidal bent in sexual perversions.

So much said for the roots of much of the British Royal breeding as such since that time!

This set of developments flowing from the role of the psycho-pathologically impaired Henry VIII, was employed by a cabal of Venetian agents, led by Venice's Francesco Zorzi, to drive a wedge between Henry VIII and the Catholic Church. This occurred at a time, after the stresses of the 1492, Habsburg expulsion of the Jews from Spain, in which the conditions of peace among the leading powers of Europe were already strained to near the breaking-point, by the effects of the case of Martin Luther on the European state of affairs generally. The brainwashing of Henry VIII by his Venetian manipulators, thus became the detonator which plunged all of Europe into an epidemic, a spread of a continuing series of outbreaks of religious warfare over the entire span from the preceding, A.D. 1492 expulsion of the Jews from Spain, until the 1648 Peace of Westphalia.

The effects of this legacy of a clinically "failed personality," this time, were represented, not by President Obama, but by Henry VIII's Venice-evoked state of public insanity. These developments represented not only a general breakdown of systems corresponding to the ecumenical goals of Cardinal Nicholas of Cusa himself, and of the great ecumenical Council of Florence as well; these types of pathetic developments which are merely typified by the case of Henry VIII, remain the root-cause of all of the greatest of all the crises of European civilization to the present time.[18]

So, just as Cardinal Nicholas of Cusa had assessed the situation within Europe, as having been degenerated into a general state of the European system at the relevant time; so, slightly more than a century after,

---

18. A recent dinner-table discussion with a relevant academic figure, on the subject of failed political leaders, requires a proverbial two words of caution in approaching that subject. The cases of the category of the failed personalities the Emperor Nero, Adolf Hitler, and President Barack Obama, should be clear as to fact in a way which is beyond competent question. Such cases as those also typify a certain general category of more or less identical types of cases from many walks of life. However, it would be in error to fall into the fraudulent practice of that notorious priest of the Delphi cult, Plutarch, in his dubious, facetiously motivated *The Lives of Famous Men*.

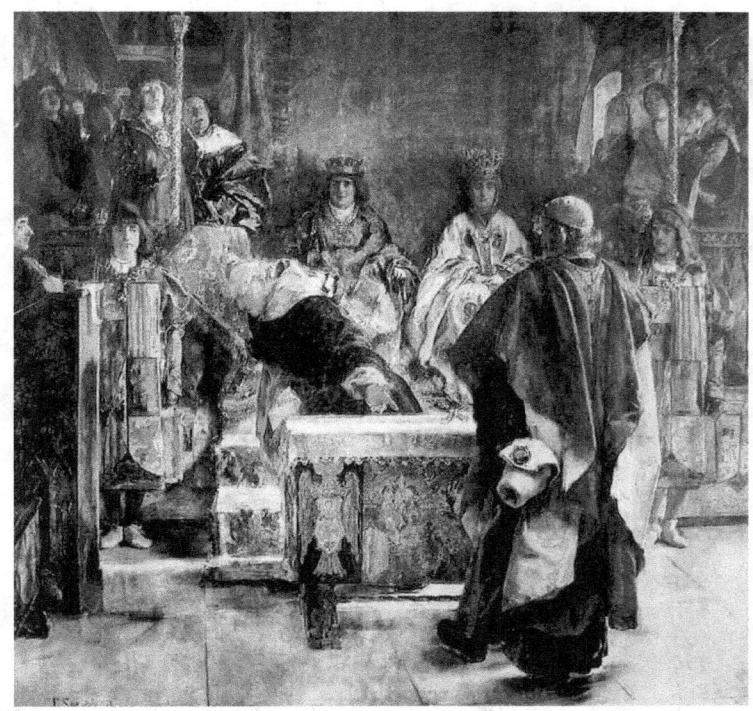

The expulsion of the Jews from Spain in 1492, was the opening shot, by the Habsburg oligarchy, of the 150-year-long religious wars, which finally ended in 1648 with the Treaty of Westphalia. Shown: The Grand Inquisitor Tomás de Torquemada offering the Edict of Expulsion of the Jews to the Catholic monarchs, Ferdinand and Isabella of Spain, 1492; by Emilio Sala (1889).

Cusa follower Christopher Columbus had acted on Cusa's proposal to reach across the oceans to continents from which the intended mission of the great Council of Florence could be relaunched into a corrupted Europe, Columbus attempted his famous, great mission.

Columbus tried, but the Habsburgs' influence over the Spanish monarchy, largely ruined the purpose of his mission. So, the effort had been launched again, later, this time as a nominally Protestant venture (!), with the Plymouth and Massachusetts Bay settlements in New England, shortly before the organization of the 1648 Peace of Westphalia by a special ecumenical mission, assigned by a Pope (!), to a person made famous as Jules Cardinal Mazarin.

Venetian monetarist Imperialism took over in Europe. There followed the decline of Venice's earlier chosen favorite for the political system of this financial-imperialist corruption in modern Europe, which was first assigned to the Habsburgs. With the accession of James I of England, a dupe of the Venetian schemes of Paolo Sarpi and the scoundrels Francis Bacon, and the latter pair's Thomas Hobbes, Anglo-Dutch-ruled Sarpian England, emerged, over the course of the Seventeenth Century, as, also, with the accession of the later Hannover monarchy, the base for the dominant role of an Anglo-Dutch world empire of the seas, which assumed the role of the Eighteenth-century, and later, British East India Company.

From the onset and aftermath of the Peloponnesian War, to the present day, European imperialism was never actually a practice of a sovereign nation-state, but, rather, of international monetarist, and related financier interests. Go back about 28,000 years, to the time that the most recent, great glaciation of the northern hemisphere began its long, slow retreat, until the level of the world's oceans rose by about 400 feet, to the present approximated levels, about 5,000 years, or somewhat more, ago.

From Out of the Oceans' Myths

The Roman Empire period's famous chronicler, Diodorus Siculus, is not entirely trusted among all relevant scholars, but the combination of his own interviews with Berbers and his re-warming of the work of Egyptian historians from earlier times, yields a picture from amid the myths of past times which does, in fact, correspond to some useful physical and other evidence bearing on the roots of modern outgrowths of the civilization of the Mediterranean maritime littoral of relevant ancient European times.

What is clearly appearing from out of the mists of those past times, is that the scientific evidence is, presently, that the Great Pyramid of Giza is the artefact of the colonization of our post-glacial European past. It is clear that all leading Mediterranean cultures of the pre-Homeric period were dominated by maritime cultures, which established a predominantly oligarchical form of rule over the relatively illiterate populations within the Mediterranean periphery.

There is a related kind of history of Mesopotamia and the once-powerful, iron-working, Hittite "Kingdom" reaching inland, from the Black Sea coast, to the north of Mesopotamia; but, to put the point briefly, the dominant cultures of the ancient Mediterranean which entered from the Atlantic region, were what is classed

creative commons

The once-powerful, iron-working Hittite kingdom, dating from the 18th Century B.C., reached inland, from the Black Sea coast, to the north of Mesopotamia. It was an exception to the ancient maritime Mediterranean, predominantly oligarchical cultures. Here, the remains of the Hittite kingdom in Anatolia.

as predominantly oligarchical cultures which may be usefully regarded as skilled navigators preying upon the already established, relatively ignorant inland populations within a maritime culture's reach of the Mediterranean itself.

Today, the ***Iliad*** and ***Odyssey,*** re-examined today, provoke us to notice some fairly chosen insights into the minds, rather than the mere sense-impressions taken from the myths and fancies presented to us by that oligarchical maritime culture.

So, for Homer, and for the accounts presented by Aeschylus, of the earlier role of those who had entered the Mediterranean as a maritime oligarchy, and who were regarded by the credulous as gods, such as that fratricidal son of Olympia himself. What we know from the period of the ancient, so-called Classical Greece and associated maritime cultures, then supplies the advantage of deep insight of the witting, into the minds of the reigning maritime cultures of the so-called Classical Greek and later times. This is especially to be noted by choosing Aeschylus' ***Prometheus Bound*** as a focal point of reference. Here we find the proof of what we know presently as the innermost secrets of the souls of the copy-cats of the ancient maritime gods and goddesses in the virtual deification of the dubious aristocrats of the British imperialist cabal.

That much said here on that point, I now return your attention to a crucial point of insight which I had freshly emphasized in an earlier chapter of this present report.

The Captain in Space, Again

During the preceding chapter, I referred your attention to the image of the commander of a sealed cabin traveling in the space filled with cosmic radiation, but with no contact with the space around him, excepting sensors whose function were equivalent to human sense-organs. That commander would depend upon the same mental processes required by Johannes Kepler's uniquely original discovery of the principle of gravitation: the resolution of two kinds of biological sensing equivalent to human sense-perception. Such was the notion of sight, and the hearing of harmonics, which were employed in ironical conjunction, for Kepler's great discovery of what Albert Einstein would later term "a finite, but not bounded universe."

Pause to refer again, briefly, to the concept of metaphor in William Empson's ***Seven Types of Ambiguity***.

The problem which continues to cripple the sense of personal identity of most persons, still today, is that they presume that they have no existence in the universe, but their presumption of an actually non-existent, but presumably self-evident truth, the presumption that those biological instruments which are being used for navigation through what are only the shadows cast by an unseen reality of the actual universe.

Our senses, and those scientific instruments which mankind has crafted to "see" beyond the limitations of our original sense-perceptual powers, are, indeed, necessary; but, neither those senses nor those supplementary instruments supply us the uniquely integral identity of the human observer, such as that pilot. The point I had made in the earlier chapter, and on occasions published earlier, has a deeper implication, to the effect of a point stressed by Gottfried Leibniz, in presenting his modern conception of *dynamics*, and by Percy Bysshe Shelley in the concluding paragraphs of his *A Defence of Poetry*.

Shelley's argument there, refers to a crucial feature of a discovery reported by Gottfried Leibniz during the course of his discoveries of physical principle, in denouncing the fraud of Rene Descartes, as he did during the concluding decade of the Seventeenth Century: Leibniz thus presented the essential physical conception of *dynamics*, or, the equivalent notion of the ancient Classical Greek *dynamis* of such as the Pythagoreans and Plato.

The same conception as that of Leibniz and Shelley (among others) on this account, provided the basis for an ostensibly spontaneous inspiration, leading to a remarkable report by Rosa Luxemburg, on the subject of what she named as "the mass strike."

Call this quality of subtle perception an expression of "prescience." It is also expressed by the prescient quality of the act of discovery of a valid universal physical principle of physical science, as Leibniz points to the implication of the "infinitesimal" of his calculus, in the course of his presentation of dynamics. It is otherwise known as the quality of human individual genius, and sometimes known, or merely believed to be, rightly, or wrongly, an act of "intuition."

Whether or not this is actually "prescience," is a distinction known to us in a secure way, only through the methods of scientific proof of principle, methods typified by the accomplishments of Brunelleschi, Cusa, Leonardo da Vinci, Johannes Kepler, et al., as these are to be judged today by the standard set, for these purposes, by Bernhard Riemann's 1854 habilitation dissertation. Yet, the same principle underlies all true conceptions of Classical artistic insight, as the case of Albert Einstein and his violin implies, and as the history of Lejeune Dirichlet's role, as a leading world scientist, among the greatest artistic personalities of the Nineteenth Century.

There are even indications of such seemingly mysterious powers of ostensibly "extra-sensory" perception in the sometimes panicked, or other herd-like behavior among beasts, under special occasions. These are not matters of "mystical powers," but are, essentially, a demonstration that the implicitly communicable powers of the healthily developed human mind are not confined to the subject-matters specific to sense-perceptions as such, as the case of Max Planck's friend Wolfgang Köhler helps to illustrate this point.

Among the best demonstrations of the principle of "prescience" we have the work of a diminishing ration of Classical musicians who are capable of recognizing the difference between performing the notes of a composition according to the principle of J.S. Bach, and those who are actually capable of fulfilling the intention of the music. The great conductor Wilhelm Furtwängler identified this by his use of the term "performing between the notes." Or, performing the appropriate choice of transitions within the performance of the music, rather than the ostensibly literal notes.

This is not arbitrary. The case of the requirements for a successful performance, according to Mozart's intention, of Mozart's **Ave Verum Corpus**, is a case in point on that account.

Mozart's composition treats the motet as equivalent to a dramatic message of inspiration. The question posed to the performer is: "Have you delivered that message?" The intent should be clear to you; therefore, read the singing of the notes accordingly, to the effect of the completion of the message projected. Have you motivated the audience to hear Mozart's message to them, through you?

Then, consider the degree to which all Classical art was corrupted, virtually beyond recognition of its composed intent, as was done by the influence of the utterly depraved, post-World War II European Congress for Cultural Freedom, or, the earlier, post-World War I German "expressionists" such as the author of the "Fur-lined Cup and Saucer" which the Dadaists presented to those privileged to pass through the 1919 pissoir of the great railway station of Cologne into the hall of the assembled depraved. The virtually decreed "popular entertainment" culture of the post-World War II trans-Atlantic community, shows the effect of such depravity, even when the composition presented was of a Classical form and intent. There has been a consequent loss of access to the creative powers of the individual mind which has been conditioned to such modes of "entertainment," like that of an intimate moment with a diseased prostitute, and to the depravity which the client delivers to his putative customer of that saddening moment.

The effect of such depravity, is a marked loss of those powers of creative insight upon which the voluntary progress of a society depends more or less absolutely. It is the agency of prescience which dwells, like all true discoveries of universal principle in physical science, essentially, outside the perceptions of our limited range of sense-certainty as such, which defines the cultural environment on which the creative powers of the mind depend for their appropriate intuition.

Reference to the large category of work on the principles of composition presented by Friedrich Schiller, as on the role of the principle of insight essential to the Classical drama, is relevant here.

Essentially, in the great dramas of Shakespeare and Schiller, or as in Eugene O'Neill's *The Iceman Cometh*, there are no actual heroes in the drama on stage. The hero, as Schiller emphasizes, is the citizen in the audience who is inspired to supply the needed hero of his or her society in oneself, by becoming a true citizen. The same could be said of the tragedies of Aeschylus. For Schiller, an immortal Jeanne d'Arc did not fail, as the history of France in that same century attests, as in the role of Louis XI. Such is the true principle of any really valid Renaissance.

To sum up the relevant aspects of this point, the ability to locate one's own identity in the influence one contributes to the benefit of future mankind, defines a special relationship which persists outside the confines of the sense-certainty of a mortal life. This bears on the true meaning of that immortality which belongs to the human individual, as no other. The body dies, but that which was, and remains immortal, such as the original discovery of a great principle of nature, or of valid Classical art, lives on.

It is a lack of grasp of that aspect of the creative powers developed in the human individual, which is the source of the temptations of immorality, and of the sordid temptations of the failed personality. This immortality is specific to the expression of a true discovery of the quality of universal principle which Aristotle claimed to present, but did not; whereas, the depraved dupes of the British empiricist mathematicians' school of Paolo Sarpi and Bertrand Russell deny the existence of any and all actual universal principles in the physical universe, but claim, like the depraved, poor dead souls of that special Hell known as the Laxenberg, Austria International Institute for Applied Systems Analysis (IIASA), to recognize only "mathematical" physics, not the real kind.

The relevance of Classical art to science as defined for modern life by Bernhard Riemann's 1854 habilitation dissertation, lies in this distinction. This is a matter which I am prepared to take up at this point.

Physical Economy as Science

What blinds even most seriously qualified economists to the essential reality of the present global economic-breakdown-crisis currently under way, is the notion that economic forecasting and related subject-matters must be conducted with primarily mathematical emphasis on a money-system as such.

The essential correction to be made, as of urgent relevance at this time of great crisis in world history, is to insist that the study of actual economic processes can not be based competently on ontologically mathematical systems, such as money schemes comparable to the current Wall Street board-game of an absolutely lunatic, run-amok form of real-life pursuit of a merely virtual game of "Monopoly."

My own adopted profession, since early 1953, has been that of a physical economist in the Bernhard Riemann school of physical scientific methods, and a specialist in treating economic processes, not as in terms of so-called quantities of "energy," but as located in the increase, or decline of *potential energy-flux-density* as our work of the 1970s and 1980s, rooted then in the Fusion Energy Foundation (FEF) emphasized, in respect to what would have succeeded as the initiative through which I brought into being what President Ronald Reagan named the proposed U.S.A.-Soviet Strategic Defense Initiative (SDI).[19] The relevant definitions required must be located, as I would presume, with re-enforced confidence, in recent times, in a notion consistent with a universal system of cosmic radiation defined in terms of singularities, rather than discrete particles, as a proper, corrective treatment of the famous Louis de Broglie paradox implies, as Albert Einstein's relevant work implies.

This means, on one level, a general notion of chemical potential as defined in respect to the conventional view of the Periodic Table of chemistry. On a higher level the role of nuclear fission enters. On a still-higher level, the role of thermonuclear fusion enters. Beyond that, the question posed pertains to the name of "matter/anti-matter reactions."

This view requires the included discipline of casting aside the popularized fraud known as "The Second Law of Thermodynamics" as introduced by Rudolf Clausius, et al. From the standpoint of any competent physical economist, the entire universe must be considered

---

19. The SDI, which I personally initiated in fact during the late 1970s, was adopted as a project by relevant leading, highly qualified circles of both military and scientific figures of nations such as Germany, France, Italy, and others, and spread quickly once I had entered into cooperation on this project with relevant officials of both the U.S.A. and Soviet governments during the early years of the U.S. Presidency of Ronald Reagan.

as a whole as essentially anti-entropic, as Albert Einstein's characterization of Kepler's discovery implies: the universe is implicitly finite, but, because this involves a general principle of universal anti-entropy, is never bounded.

Throw all that rubbish associated with the cult of Bertrand Russell out, including the intellectual waste-matter produced by the creatively inert, Russellite devotees of the International Institute for Applied Systems Analysis (IIASA).

As to economics itself, the following summary is required here.

Take my often-repeated, pedagogical case, that of the illustrative case of iron ore. We seek the richest lodes, which were usually assembled within the bodies of deceased living plants or creatures which gather iron into their bodies. When we mine what are the economically acceptable concentrations of that that ore, we reduce the richness of the concentration of that ore in a way which converges on a critical form of physical-economic problem. However, generally speaking, the iron remains within the possession of our planet; it has been only relatively dispersed in a way which converges on economic limits of the economy at that level of development. Costs and correlated problems increase accordingly. Therefore, compensating progress, as in the mode of increase of applicable energy-flux density, is required to offset that rise in cost of extraction and concentration. This requires an offsetting increase of the applied energy-flux density, without which a present civilization toying foolishly with such silly practices as "solar" and "wind" power, such as a "cap and trade" lunacy, would be threatened with foreseeably deep genocidal degrees of collapse of potential relative population-density planet-wide.

Such has been the experience of the advances of society.

Although the action of probably polarized fusion in the vicinity of the Sun, had produced most of the higher parts of the periodic table among the planets, the idea of limiting the rise of potential energy-flux density to the relatively non-nuclear fission regions among the planets, compels us to seek to reach the increases in energy-flux density which are needed to free mankind from the limits attributable to a simple notion of the formerly traditional periodic table. Hence, nuclear-fission, and thermonuclear fusion are absolutely required for man's continued progress at this stage in human existence on Earth. The latter requirements are, presently, variously relative, or absolute.

Next, after considering the primary aspects of the required role of increases of the energy-flux-density of society considered as a whole, we must consider that level as being the general driver on which the level of energy-flux density applied to infrastructure and production depends, however, at a lower level than the primary sources for the economic system as a whole.

In all cases, it is the relatively anti-entropic level of action which is the primary determinant of progress or entropy of the economic system as a whole.

What, Then Happens to Money?

Under the "Hamiltonian" kind of physical-economy system which I specify as the absolutely indispensable, immediate reform in the world's current economic system, money does not suddenly disappear. Rather, it assumes the quality of credit uttered by sovereign nation-state institutions. In a healthy form and practice of a modern sovereign nation-state, the authority for creating credit is restricted to sovereign nation-state governments. In the market at large, the principal channel of circulation of nation-state-uttered credit is the merchant banking-system according to the original Glass-Steagall Act *as if it had never been repealed!* This feature of an international body of cooperating, sovereign nation-states, requires a fixed-exchange-rate system of world credit among the array of sovereign nation-states.

It may look like money, but when you try to spend it, it behaves according to its true nature, as state-uttered credit circulating within a world system of sovereign nation-states operating under fixed-exchange-rate rules.

Such a new system could be started now "as if on a dime." It is probably the only action sufficient to halt the presently accelerating plunge of the entire planet into a prolonged "new dark age."

Under such a system, the most relevant physical principle, is that the level of potential represented by the operating energy-flux density "at the level of production," reflects the higher order of physical-chemical potential represented by the primary source of physical power used to drive the potential of the lower order of components of the economy as a whole.

As for the speculative banks excluded from participating in the credit supplied by government through aid of the credit entrusted to a merchant-banking system, the speculative institutions are "on their own resources," to sink or swim, as nature might provide.

IV. The Tragedy of Long Wars

So much now said on background, I resume my earlier emphasis on the implicit originality of the subject of the Peloponnesian War, a war properly classified as "a chronic war of a maritime culture," an ancient such war akin to the modern European 1756-63 "Seven Years War," a war which was exploited at that time, to establish the British East India Company as a virtually world empire on its own account.

For the purposes of presenting this chapter's summary of the subject-matter of the report as a whole, the specific set of "chronic wars" considered now, is limited to the relevant set of those wars which were organized, since the sequence of Thermopylae and Salamis, from both within Europe and the adjoining littoral of the Mediterranean. This includes an emphasis on such cases as the chronic, modern European warfare of A.D. 1492-1648 and the British authorship of so-called "World Wars" #1 and #2, wars which had been concocted by the British Empire for the purpose of either establishing, or maintaining imperial power over the relevant set of what should have been, by their nature, sovereign nation-states.

On the subject of the contrast between "necessary" and "bad" wars in modern, globally extended European history, which is to say since approximately A.D. 1401, we must say have the following here.

Cusa Is Crucial

As the then contemporary evidence known to Cardinal Nicholas of Cusa had emphasized, the religious warfare of 1492-1648, had been launched under Venetian impetus, for the purpose of Venice's determination to ruin the great reform which had been established within Europe, as established by the A.D. 1438-39 Council of Florence. There arose a Habsburg-led form of what would become known later, properly, as "fascism," then in the form of the Inquisition led by Spain's evil, Grand Inquisitor. This development was expressed then, in the conflict between the contrary developments of, on the one side, Christopher Columbus's successful trans-Atlantic voyage, in Columbus' role as an explicit follower of the strategic policy of Cusa, and, on the opposing side, what turned out to have been the Habsburg Inquisition's expulsion of the Jews from Spain. The Venetian control of England's Henry VIII, in breaking the peace among those principal powers which were Spain, France, and England, turned the already murderous conflict which dominated the remainder of the period of 1492-1648 into general religious warfare throughout Europe.

The chief precedent for the pattern of ancient through modern chronic states of warfare centered within the region of the Mediterranean, has been, variously, to establish, or to maintain, an imperial reign over those nations or comparable regions.

Thus, out of that development, came the accession of the Anglo-Dutch William of Orange. All specifically *chronic* wars since that time, have been orchestrated by London-centered, financial-imperialist interests, according to the intended benefit of building, maintaining, taking over, or imitating the British Empire, all that as an echo of the practices of chronic warfare by the ancient Roman Empire, or Byzantine empire earlier. The British imperial ideology is the most essential expression of imperialism throughout all parts of the planet presently. That is what is presently continued as the British monarchy's imperial intent to destroy the sovereignty of the respective nations of modern Europe, and, most emphatically, the power which the British empire fears the most, the U.S.A.'s potentially infectious system of constitutional republicanism.

In that larger historical context, of the rise and persistence of what became today's British imperialism, the Israeli-Arab wars and related homicide, combined with the wars against Iraq and among the British drug pushers of the opium fields of Afghanistan, are typical, as evil, as we should recognize in U.S. President Barack Obama's promoting the needless deaths of U.S. soldiers in protecting the British opium traffic out of the poppy-fields of Afghanistan. With the wasting of the lives and ruined living bodies of U.S. military personnel in this operation, there is featured a practice which is reminiscent of the British monarchy's deploying the evil Nineteenth-century Spanish monarchy for the trafficking of African slaves into the Americas, and for the creation of the British monarchy's puppet, the Confederate States of America, both as part of the (fortunately failed) intention of the British monarchy to destroy our United States forever.

The chronic warfare continued in the general area of

Among the long wars that have bedeviled mankind over the past several millennia, were the Napoleonic Wars (1799-1815). The horror of those wars, especially as they overran Spain, was captured in a series of etchings and paintings by the great Spanish painter Goya; here, from the series, "The Disparates," the "Folly of Fear" (ca. 1815-24).

the British-controlled Near-East, Sykes-Picot region, including the British, opium-centered aspect of the chronic warfare conducted, in British interest, in its assigning the U.S. role in the war conducted by U.S. puppet-President Barack Obama in Afghanistan and adjoining locations, is, like the pattern of the behavior of Britain's Israeli puppet, typical of that phenomenon in the British imperialism's Sykes-Picot region.

The root of this specifically imperialist pattern in chronic warfare, may be located in the origins of the Delphi-based Olympian Apollo-Dionysus cult's role in the orchestration of the Peloponnesian War, and in that evil, Delphic role, which an evil Aristotle played up through the time of the death of the Alexander the Great. So, the great tragedian Aeschylus had warned of such Olympian evil of Delphi in his own *Prometheus Trilogy*.

To repeat the point which I have made on this account earlier within this report, it was the maritime class which was the real-life expression of the maritime tyranny of the legendary gods of Olympus. The power exerted by that class was one of a social formation whose real-life center of maritime monetary power, was that cult of Delphi whose last leading priest, and prototype of the later monetarist power of Venice, was

imperial Rome's ever-lying high priest of the cult of Delphi, Plutarch.

To summarize those pertinent highlights of the immediately preceding summary, what I have presented at this outset of this present chapter, the characteristic feature of the historical process which led into, and out of the Peloponnesian War, had produced a monetarist form of international maritime power, centered in the relevant Mediterranean maritime ports. That is continued, as the British empire of the present time.

But, we must call attention to a certain qualitative change.

British Maritime Power

Under the evolution of that maritime-imperialist intention, the effect of the development of a strategic quality of trans-Atlantic maritime interest, the "center of gravity" of European maritime imperialism shifted, from emphasis on the Mediterranean, to emphasis on the Atlantic. With that shift, within the Venetian monetary oligarchy, from the Mediterranean to the Atlantic, the so-called "geopolitical" orientations among the nations of the European continent shifted. The shift from a strategic center-of-gravity in the Mediterranean, to the Atlantic, led to a new Venetian imperial strategy, that of shifting the strategic command post for operations against continental Europe and the Mediterranean littoral, to the North Atlantic maritime bases in the British Isles and watery maritime site of the Netherlands. Hence the late Nineteenth-century arrays of geopolitical conflict.

From the outset, already in A.D. 1620 New England, especially since the launching of the Massachusetts Bay colony under the leadership of the Winthrops and Mathers, that for as long as the original Royal charter reigned, the Venetian policy for its Anglo-Dutch maritime puppet, was expressed in, first, the manipulations of France's Louis XIV, and, with the successful ruin of France through the manipulations of the Bourbon monarchies of Louis XIV-Louis XVI, and of defacto British puppet Napoleon Bonaparte, a specifically

British, but Venice-controlled, imperial power, was established through the agency of the so-called "Seven Years War." This "Seven Years War" became, thus, the font from which have flowed all the principal horrors of the planet's imperialist "long wars" ever since.

The "Seven Years War," which established the relatively independent, Venetian-style power of the notorious British East India Company, from February 1763 onward, established the principled, recurring role of long wars radiating throughout the world, since that time, to the present date. This became the currently operating pattern of "chronic long wars" within the international community, since that time, since the death of England's Queen Anne, to the present day.

As under the role of the ancient Roman Empire within the Mediterranean, chronic warfare modeled upon the precedent of the Babylonian, Persian, and Roman empires, has been the essential, characteristic feature of imperialist practice, from the Peloponnesian War, to the present role of British imperialism in world affairs today. The significant change of character within imperialism considered in the large, a change from a Mediterranean, to an Atlantic maritime culture, has been the principal distinction of the Asian, from the Mediterranean modes of imperialism.

The difference between the Asian and European models of imperialism, is that with the exception of a certain part of the history of what became known as India, maritime culture since the lifetime of Egypt's great Eratosthenes, until the successive development of inland canal systems unleashed by Charlemagne, and the canal-like supranational railway systems, European-based maritime imperialism since the rise of Greek-centered maritime culture in the Mediterranean, has been the only known long-term form of society capable of superceding the Asian imperialist models.

Thus, the root of that practice of imperialism, has remained monetarism, from the fall of the Asian-based empires, to the present day.

Ending the Reign of Monetarism

From the beginning of European imperialism, the idea of a value intrinsic to money, has been the companion and implicit origin of European maritime modes of imperialism. It signifies the reign of a form of political power, money, which is independent of the authority of any nation-state.

The usual source of confusion on this point, as among Europeans and nearly all of the citizens of the United States, too, is a lack of a sense of the distinction between two apparently similar, but, actually, mutually exclusive notions of the ontological import of a nation's uttered currency.

For example, since Roman imperial times, it was understood that the authority to define law, was not granted to a king, but only to an emperor, such as Caesar. A king had the power to make decisions, but not law. This arrangement under Roman imperial rule, was an echo of the supra-national power expressed as the will of those virtual maritime pirates, the collective image of an imperial Olympian Zeus, who exerted a supranational power over the unfortunate landlubbers of the coasts and mainland interior.

To get to the essence of this distinction, consider the role of scrip ("The Pinetree Shilling") uttered as a form of credit for as long as Massachusetts enjoyed the sovereignty which had been conceded by Royal Charter to the Massachusetts colony *for as long as that Charter remained in force*.

In fact, for all of the sophistry taught by pompous academic fools, and their popular, or otherwise pompous likenesses, as taught to their gaping-mouthed credulous, assembled dupes in the classroom, the only real economic value is a certain kind of physical value which is rooted in the physical effects of the human creation of physical wealth through production by human beings. However, this notion of a physical principle of wealth, has nothing to do with the notorious Physiocratic concoctions of the followers of François Quesnay, or to the all too trusting A.R.J. Turgot from whose papers Adam Smith plagiarized much of Smith's own *The Wealth of Nations*.

All competent notions of economic wealth are premised on forms of social practice of economy which are unique to that aspect of the nature of the human species, a nature which has no replications among the animals or plants.

Contrary to fools and scoundrels such as the professional poisoner Aristotle, the universe is essentially anti-entropic, and so is the voluntary capacity uniquely specific to the human individual will. Nature itself is ruthlessly anti-entropic on this account, but only the human individual has been shown to exert that capability by personal individual will, as this is done in the act of discovery of a true universal physical principle which is then employed to inform relevant human behavior.

I repeat a point I have frequently delivered on this account.

Take the case of the relatively rich iron-ore deposits by the shores of some parts of the Great Lakes. How did the rich deposit of iron ore get there, in the first place?

It was deposited by the dead bodies of living creatures, creatures which had inhabited that region, and had left that deposit of collected iron-ore behind. Such have been the case for most of the useful concentrations of elements of the Periodic Table on which certain important degrees of productivity have depended.

Thus, when we had relatively exhausted those deposits, it cost us more effort to secure the iron (for example) which society required. Thus, it is only through scientific and technological progress that mankind is enabled to more than offset the attrition incurred by "using up" a relatively rich lode.

This progress is accomplished, chiefly, through the effects of willful scientific progress, a progress which depends upon a combined effect of both an increase in the relative energy-flux density in the sources of power employed, and also a correlated increase of the relative capital-intensity, and increase of the physical standard of living of the population.

Like the Prometheus of Aeschylus, who challenged the Olympian gods, and stole their fire to give to mankind, so our ancestors came to these shores, to bring progress, through science and Classical culture, safely away from the oligarchical pestilence of Europe. Here, ships arrive with Pilgrim settlers in Salem Harbor, 1628.

Prometheus Bound!

Aeschylus' **Prometheus Trilogy** is to be read as a case of true-to-life-life fiction. The pagan gods, such as those associated with the name of an Olympian Zeus, reigned as imperial gods, or, as half-breed demi-gods, over a mass of virtual slaves. The slaves were not permitted to know, or to practice technologies other than those of their slavish grandfathers, and the grandfathers' grandfathers, before them. Prometheus pled for the right of those oppressed human beings to enjoy the rights which had been usurped by the tyrannical Olympian gods and demi-gods.

So, the people, such as our ancestors who are typified by the founding of the Chartered Massachusetts Bay Colony, took the power to progress, through science and Classical culture, to gain, thus, those estates which the tyrants had considered reserved to those tyrants and other wastrels who considered themselves virtually as gods. So, despite the crushing, by the British tyrant, of the Massachusetts Bay Colony's original human rights, they provoked those of us inspired by that colony's example, to create a higher form of government on these shores.

So, also, the lackeys of tyrants propose to reverse the tide of scientific progress in technologies of production, and to condemn the resort to higher forms of that fire we call energy-flux-density. Such are the slaves, who would kill neighbors who refuse to assume the shackles of brutishness which the so-called "environmentalists" have demanded they wear.

In the meanwhile, the ogre of a British Empire lurks and prowls with vast homicide in mind, to make the people stupid, through the kinds of technologies and public education and public health programs as which President Obama prescribes.

This is done by so-called Malthusian measures, which the British monarchy baldly asserts must be done to lower the human population of the planet, and that quickly, from about 6.7 billions persons, to a monstrously ignorant and brutish, greatly stupefied, far, far less than two. Such are the health-care and related policies which the British Blair ministry has passed on to the British lackey known as the Obama Presidency.

Helga Zepp-LaRouche Sets The Record Straight on Helmut Kohl

German Chancellor Helmut Kohl speaks at the official opening of the Brandenburg Gate on Dec. 22, 1989.

EDITORIAL

June 19—The Chairwoman of the German Schiller Institute, Helga Zepp-LaRouche, wrote the following statement for the EIR *Strategic Alert Service on June 18, two days after the passing of Helmut Kohl, of the Christian Democratic Union (CDU), who was Chancellor of Germany from 1982 to 1998, which included the period of its reunification.*

The various assessments of Helmut Kohl as the "father of German unity" and "the visionary of a united Europe" sound more like the PR description of the politically correct understanding that Kohl's contemporaries are supposed to have of that historical period, which coincided with his term in office. But the story of the geopolitical operations that targetted Kohl, in particular, during the time of German reunification, have been totally suppressed. These operations are still playing out to this day in other forms.

It is to Kohl's credit that, with the release of his "Ten Point Plan for a Confederation of the two Germanys" on Nov. 28, 1989, he made a first baby step toward establishing German sovereignty, a step which he had not coordinated with the Allies or with his coalition partner, the then Foreign Minister Hans-Dietrich Genscher, of the Free Democratic Party (FDP).

A truthful picture must include the fact that the assassination two days later of Alfred Herrhausen, then-chairman of Deutsche Bank and a close advisor to Kohl, allegedly by the third generation of the Red Army Faction (RAF), was meant to immediately contain this impulse to obtain sovereignty.

What is also omitted in the many comments is Margaret Thatcher's hate-filled "Fourth Reich" campaign against Kohl, as well as François Mitterrand's threats of war in the event Kohl were not ready to abandon the deutschemark sovereign currency as the price to pay for reunification, and to accept the constraints of the Maastricht Treaty straitjacket and the euro, as reported by Jacques Attali in his biography of Mitterrand.

Kohl later described the European Community Summit in early December 1989 in Strasbourg, where he faced these attacks, as one of the darkest hours of his life. According to his own statements, it was not until his Dec. 19, 1989 visit to Dresden, with the population shouting "Helmut! Helmut!" with joy, that he realized that the moment for German reunification had come.

Of course, Helmut Kohl was also a living witness to the promise made by the Americans to Mikhail Gorbachov, as was reported by then U.S. Ambassador to the Soviet Union, Jack Matlock, among others, that NATO would never expand up to Russia's borders. For Kohl, the Cold War had ended with the breakup of the Soviet Union, and it is highly doubtful that he would have agreed with the demonization of Vladimir Putin of the past years. The fact that Mrs. Merkel now considers herself as the proconsul of Barack Obama's policy of confrontation would probably also not be to his liking.

No Piecemeal Infrastructure Approach Possible: USA Requires New Paradigm

by Diane Sare

EDITORIAL

June 20—As at least 1.5 million commuters are already aware, what New York Governor Andrew Cuomo has called the "Summer of Hell" begins on July 10. If leading officials in the New York Metropolitan area do not quickly change the way they are thinking about the rail and tunnel situation, it will truly become hellish, in ways they cannot even imagine. At issue is a tunnel and rail system that is more than a century old, which moves millions of people in and out of Manhattan every day. After derailments in early April, it became clear that repairs to the tracks at Penn Station could no longer be delayed, so these urgently needed repairs are set to begin on July 10. This means a reduction in the number of trains entering Penn Station, which will affect Long Island and New Jersey commuters, who will have to find alternative routes to get into the city.

There's the Rub!

Since necessary action on the overall rail grid has been so long delayed, and what has actually been done has been squeezed to miniscule proportions due to budget constraints and small-mindedness, there is no redundancy in alternative routes that can accommodate a 20% increase in commuters. The rush-hour traffic by car is already intense; the bus lanes through Lincoln Tunnel are at or above maximum capacity; and the same is true for the other rail lines. Governor Cuomo is reportedly trying to make emergency repairs on crumbling roads to handle the extra automobile traffic, and in New Jersey, Morris County and Essex County commuters will be rerouted to the PATH train's Hoboken station, but these trains are also already at or over capacity as well.

In April 2019, the L train line will be closed for 15 months to repair the Canarsie Tunnel, damaged by Hurricane Sandy in 2012. A proposal to reroute the G Train to help address this problem was shot down by MTA representatives, who say that there are already too many trains using the proposed alternative line. What no one is saying straight out, is that we have reached the end. That is, there is no redundancy. The entire system is at the breaking point, and closing one section for repair or maintenance risks pushing another section over the limit. Better for half of New York City to just take a two-month vacation somewhere else. Helga Zepp-LaRouche pointed out today, that unless there is a comprehensive plan to solve this, and people are informed of it, there will be chaos and potential upheaval.

There are already hints of such chaos as the overloaded system groans on—even before the scheduled reductions in service. In early June, a subway car got stuck in a tunnel and the temperatures inside became sauna-like, while the passengers waited for 45 minutes for the train to move. Now, passengers are breaking out of stalled trains and walking on the tracks to get to work—an extremely dangerous proposition.

The Solution for Tomorrow—Today

A few weeks ago, Lyndon LaRouche called for assembling a committee to put forward a solution to this crisis. That committee is being assembled. This problem cannot be addressed through public-private partnerships and piecemeal, localized plans. China is building transcontinental, high-speed rail corridors in Asia, South America, and Africa. We must think like the Chinese, and join their Belt and Road Initiative. As we develop real high-speed rail—that is, trains that travel at 250 mph—Boston and Philadelphia will become part of this region. New York City will be the center of it. The new tracks and stations must be planned to serve a vibrant region of East Coast commuters for at least 50 years into the future. Adding sky lights and shopping centers to Penn Station will do nothing, except waste time and money.

The only way to fund an infrastructure program on the scale that is needed, is in the way that Lyndon LaRouche has proposed in his Four Laws. First and foremost, stop the hemorrhaging with Glass-Steagall. No more trillion-dollar "quantitative easing" (QE) packages; that money is worthless! The banks must be separated by function—that is, solvent commercial and savings & loan banks must be separated from speculative investment banks. That step must be followed immediately by the creation of a top-down system of national banking and credit, as President Abraham Lincoln did with his successful Greenback policy.

The purpose of such a Federal Credit System is to increase the productivity of the American people, through investment in, and development of advanced technologies, which will also create mass employment in new, productive jobs. Jobs which can become ca-

reers, as opposed to taking in each other's laundry, as millions are now doing with the informal, app-based, slave-labor economy of today.

Finally, all of this must be driven by a commitment to harnessing thermonuclear fusion power to supply mankind's ever-increasing need for energy. Not only will a modern rail grid require an abundance of electricity, but moving mankind into space, to learn the secrets of the universe, and develop breakthroughs in science, means developing nuclear-powered rockets as President Kennedy envisioned.

Since New Yorkers are known for being outspoken, cosmopolitan, and impassioned individuals, it is unlikely that they will sit passively on the sidelines as everything breaks down. If this passion can be focussed properly, on working with President Trump to implement his campaign slogan, "Make America Great Again," and through American system methods, as LaRouche has proposed, the summer may well be hell, but the knowledge that a better future will result from current difficulties will avert complete chaos. On the other hand, if leading officials persist in their foolishly small-minded, money-worshipping state of denial exhibited thus far, expect a very hot summer of chaos and upheaval, with no end in sight. It's up to you.